Grace

To: Rev. Dr. Doris F. Abram

From: Dr. Ted Whitely

11-29-19
Friday @ his book signing
@ Gracy's home = Butch giving
tribute to Ted. Ted spoke for about 30 minutes
then he had a (question/answer)
period RIT his current book on
African american ministry
Topics. Refreshments were served
Rev. Imoke was present. A good time
was had by all present. Mark, cara,
+ adam as well as myself was present.

# - -20 I read this book for the 2nd
time without stopping. & I am proud of you Ted.

A Dissertation
Entitled

# AFRICAN AMERICAN MINISTRY TOPICS

Submitted as partial fulfillment of the requirements for
The Doctor of Philosophy in African
American Ministry (P.H.D.)

Dr. Keith Wilhite

Advisor:

Prepared for Newburgh Theological Seminary and
College of the Bible

THEODORE D. WHITELY, SR.

authorHOUSE®

*AuthorHouse™*
*1663 Liberty Drive*
*Bloomington, IN 47403*
*www.authorhouse.com*
*Phone: 1 (800) 839-8640*

*Published by AuthorHouse 10/02/2019*

*ISBN: 978-1-7283-2900-0 (sc)*
*ISBN: 978-1-7283-2899-7 (e)*

# CONTENTS

# INTRODUCTION

This dissertation is primarily written for the concerns of African American Ministry. I will discuss topics relating to the African American Church. In addition to that its history and the struggles of African Americans living in a culture that has oppressed African Americans for years. Finally, I will share positive contributions of African Americans from a theological and social stand point. In my reading and research of African Americans, the Black Church has been a positive institution of strength and survival for African Americans. Living in an environment that crushes our being of self-worth denies us of equal opportunity to even exist. As African Americans, we have relied ourselves to worship, and believe in God as our Emancipator. Proper citing is listed.

No one has the power to pull us out of slavery, insults, threats, and anything that robs us of our identity, but God. This God is the God of Abraham, Isaac, and Jacob. This God is the God of Sarah, Rebecca, and Rachel. This God is the God of the Disciples. This God is the God of Jesus Christ who is our Rock and Redeemer. I am glad that this God is the God of all Creation. It makes no difference whether we are black, white, red, or yellow, he is our God. Worshipping God in the Black Church gives us freedom to sing, pray, shout, speak in tongues, and other expressions of worship. It is hard to do all of those forms of worship in a hostile environment.

Over the years, and even now, we are a blessed people because God has brought us a long way. We have made many strides of success, but we are not where we really want to be. Perfectness comes when we have the fullness of Christ in us and we show our faith in his perfectness. This only happens when we meet our heavenly home. "Take away an accident of pigmentation of... our outer skin and there is no difference between me and anyone else said by Shirley Chisholm."

The church today, existing in a highly competitive, often critical society, can't thrive and be effective only when its members are such. Whatever an individual wants his church to become he must himself be. If it is to be a spiritual haven he must be personally spiritual as said by G. Othell Hand. The solutions to some of our problems today are no more complex than they may have been at any point in human history. "People together, the young and the old, relating to one another, giving and taking, working and building together is the story of the human family and always will be as told by Thomas A. Peters."

The sayings by Chisholm, Hand and Peters comes from the book entitled, **"The Darker Brother" by James A. Warner A Visual Book/ E.P. Dutton & Co., / New York /1974** There are no page numbers in this book, it is mostly pictures, and sayings. In preparation of the African American Ministry Topics I must remind myself not to get caught up too much in my blackness where it turns me away from who I really am. I am a child of God most importantly. I must also realize that God is a Spirit and we that worship him shall worship him in spirit and in truth. If I condemn white people or other ethnicities, I'm only condemning myself. We are all of the human family. I am reminded of this saying that I learned in high school. "Heat not a furnace for your foe so hot That it does singe yourself. This is by William Shakespeare."

I lift up this prayer as I prepare this dissertation. Lord help me to realize that I am nothing without you. Thank you, Jesus, for all people whether they are black, brown, white, red, or yellow. I love them all. I know I see your face in them. Help them to see You in me. I know, God, that Your love is far beyond my imagination. Thank You God that wherever I go, whatever happens, I will never lose Your love. Because You first loved me. Amen. This holds us together.

# CHAPTER 1

# Black Church/ Spirituals and Gospels

### Topics Relating to the African American Church

Speaking of the African American Church I have learned that we have seven major historic denominations. They are the African Methodist Episcopal (A.M.E.) Church; the African Methodist Episcopal Zion (A.M.E. Zion) Church; the Christian Methodist Episcopal (C.M.E.) Church; the National Baptist Convention, U.S.A; Incorporated (N.B.C.); the National Baptist Convention of America, Unincorporated (N.B.C.A.) the Progressive National Baptist Convention (P.N.B.C.); and the Church of God in Christ (C.O.G.I.C) There is a new African American Church called the Full Gospel. I am told that more than 80 percent of all black Christians are in these denominations. It appears to me that the majority of the Protestant community in the United States has not paid very much serious attention to the exercise of faith and practice in African American life.

Is it because of the lack of interest in religious life period? We are living in the 21$^{st}$ century where emails, social media, smart phones, satellites, and other electronics get in the way of religious life. Perhaps we need to sing more. We sung years ago. What happened to our songs? Rev. Otis Moss, Jr. the pastor of Olivet Institutional Baptist Church of Cleveland Ohio quoted, "Those who did not understand African theology and African spirituality sought to silence this drum beat and jail the song leaders like the prophetic James Bevel and the gifted vocalist Bernice Johnson Reagan. Each generation must sing its song, but if we are to sing with power and purpose, we must know the songs of our ancestors and embrace the spirit of their songs. It is incomprehensible to think of Dr. King as the leader of a song less movement. African and African American theology has never been and never will be a song less theology."[1] Paul says in Ephesians 5:19 "as you sing psalms and hymns and spiritual songs among yourselves, singing and making melody to the Lord in your hearts." (New Revised Standard Version) I believe that all of God's people have a reason to sing for joy. Sometimes we are not always singing, we should be always giving thanks. Always giving thanks, even in trials and afflictions, and for all things; being satisfied of their loving intent, and good tendency. The Apostle Paul wrote to the Ephesians primarily for them to mature in their faith. He wanted them and expected that this community of faith would walk in accordance with its heavenly calling.

Paul's writing somewhere between AD 60-62 was while he was in prison in Rome. There are four Prison Epistles. They are Philippians, Colossians, Philemon and of course Ephesians. I ask myself how did Paul have the passion to encourage others to sing while he was in prison? To answer that question, I would say that Paul got his passion from the Holy Spirit. Speaking of any ethnic group that experiences prison environments need some relief to deviate from negative environments. The African American people have been exploited, held hostage as slaves, denied equal opportunity, and other forms of institutionalized racism. In spite of all this a song in their hearts has kept them spiritually strong for centuries.

I am reminded of the African American William Farley Smith who was a Methodist minister and a composer of African American songs. He was born in 1941 and died in 1997. The following song depicts that we as African Americans do sing.

### I'm Gonna Sing Traditional pg. 81 Songs of Zion

1.  I'm gon'na sing when the Spirit says Sing
    I'm gon-na sing when the Spirit says a-Sing,

I'm gon-na sing when the Spirit says a-Sing, - And o-bey the
Spir-it of the Lord.
2. shout 3. preach 4. pray 5. sing

The above song comes from the **Songs of Zion** hymnal printed
in 1981 by the Abingdon Press in Nashville Tennessee. The African
Americans continue to sing. As centuries go on we are burdened in
many ways of suffering. Without suffering, there is no progress as
shared by Frederick Douglas. If there is no cross, there is no crown
as shared by William Penn. We can give the Lord the highest praise
by shouting Hallelujah and give him Glory. This reminds me of the
song "Glory, Glory, Hallelujah" written by J. Jefferson Cleveland.
This song is also from the **Songs of Zion** hymnal. The song goes
like this.

### Glory, Glory, Hallelujah Traditional pg. 98 Songs of Zion

1.  Glory, glory, __ hal-le-lujah! Since I laid my burden down.
2.  I feel better so much better . . .
3.  Feel like shouting "Hallelujah!" . . .
4.  I am climbing Jacob's ladder . . .
5.  Ev'ry round goes higher and higher

The songs speak for themselves and both have a theological
message. The first song I'm Gonna Sing tells us that the Holy Spirit
encourages us to sing. The Holy Spirit also encourage us to shout,
preach, pray, and sing again. When we do all of those things as
African Americans, and all races of people we are truly blessed.
God wants us to do all of those things in order to give him glory.
God is a jealous God, so therefore He wants all of our attention.
The second song Glory, Glory, Hallelujah talks about what to do
since I laid my burden down. What is the burden? Whatever the
burden is, we give the Lord glory and the highest praise because He
is our burden barrier. He will take our burdens away whatever they
are. When we take our burdens to the Lord and leave them there,

we let God be God. However, when we leave the burden(s) with ourselves it escalates and get worse. We have to let go and let God.

It is a blessing that African Americans can rely on Negro Spirituals to keep their minds focused upon the spirituality of God. Spirituals emanated from the heart of the ante-bellum Negro slave as forceful outflowing's of religious passion. It is not known exactly when these powerful songs begin to spring forth; however, history confirms the use of these songs as the music of the pre-Civil War "invisible church."[2] Wyatt Tee Walker states that Spiritual music form . . .. developed as an integral part of worship in these 'invisible' churches. In the preliterate era of slavery, the fuel of the 'invisible church' was the musical expression constantly fed by the oral tradition" (19:31-32).[3]

The oral tradition of the African Americans was expressed by songs commonly called Negro Spirituals, jubilees, folk songs, shout songs, sorrow songs, slave songs, slave melodies, minstrel songs, and religious songs. These Negro spirituals have a deep religious feeling that it expresses. The conditions in which the slaves lived were negative and degrading. It is said that there are approximately six thousand independent spirituals that exist today. They are songs of people weary at heart. The music is celebrative because Africans celebrated important events such as marriages, births, and deaths with music. Singing these Negro spirituals shared words from the Old and New Testaments describing the suffering of the Hebrews in the Old Testament, and the suffering of Jesus in the New Testament and other celebrative expressions. Freedom from slavery was a challenge within itself. Songs such as "Deep River," "Steal Away," Swing Low, Sweet Chariot," "Didn't My Lord Deliver Daniel?" testified that the slaves would be freed from slavery and to get rid of trials and tribulations. The Black Church began to blossom in the early 1920's.

As the population exploded, there was an appreciation for the Black spirituals because its inception was in the cotton fields and in the rural setting of camp meetings where large numbers of Blacks attended. A new situation started in the early 1920's as Gospel music similar to the blues. It spread from the church to singing groups. As for an example.

**Precious Lord Thomas A. Dorsey pg. 179 Songs of Zion**

Precious Lord, take my hand, Lead me on, let me stand, I am tired, I am weak, I am worn. This song is a Historical Gospel penned by Dorsey, Kenneth Morris, Theodore Frye, just to name a few. This song reminds me of Psalm 5:8 saying, "Lead me O Lord, in your righteousness because of my enemies; make Your way straight before me." We need this guidance.

**What Shall I Render Margaret Pleasant
Douroux pg. 190 Songs of Zion**

What shall I render unto God for all his mercies? What shall I render, What shall I give? This song puts Psalm 116:12 in my mind saying What shall I return to the Lord for all His bounty to me? My return to the Lord would be to serve Him faithfully every day. Make the best of this life.

As praises go up blessings come down. God is jealous so therefore give God all of your soul.

The song by Douroux is a Modern Gospel song with such names as James Cleveland, Mahalia Jackson, Aretha Franklin, the Ward Singers, and others. Some of these groups and singers started during the fifties and sixties. The appearance of Modern Gospel did not in any way mark the demise of Historic Gospel. Both are very much in evidence, and they exist in parallel fashion with little or no problem.[4] Tony Heilbut states that "Gospel is more than music: it is one of the central experiences of Black America, a common heritage whose vitality was a means of survival in a hostile world."[5]

The Black Church is one of the most vital institutions to Blacks in this country, and the Black gospel is an important phase of that experience. It is an important part of the Black heritage; therefore, its history must be taught and respected. Almost every Black church nowadays has at least one gospel choir made up mostly of young people, and they are excellent groups. On the other hand, many young Blacks leaving churches where there is a paucity of Black music or where this music has to take a back seat to the European- style religious music. Others have formed community gospel choirs, many interdenominational.

Numerous excellent soloists, ensembles, and choirs have developed during this new emphasis on gospel music. They are exponents of what is now called contemporary or rock gospel. The most talented musicians of the world are found among them. It is amazing how the culture of the Black community can change its atmosphere with different styles of music. Some of us may not accept these changes of different styles of music. For generation to generation there is change. Some changes are good, and some changes is not so good. When we get into our comfort zones it is hard for us to change or even adapt to change. As with other types of music, the mass media and business has caused gospel music to become commercial. The recording industry is popular.

# CHAPTER 2

## African American Worship

In the article of **Ministry International Journal For Pastors September 2002**, (R. Clifford Jones) talks about African American Worship its heritage, character, and quality is a masterpiece. This article is on the internet by logging on to https://www.ministry magazine.org/…african american-worship-its-heritage-character-and-quality.html In his editorial notes he mentions that the varied cultures of the Christian world each have their beautiful and distinctive ways of worshipping, there is something uniquely enriching about African- American Christian worship. It embodies underlying patterns of thought and experience that do much to commend it to Christians everywhere anybody who has observed or participated in an African-Christian worship service will admit that there is an undeniable difference between the way American Blacks worship and the worship of other racial and ethnic groups.

Rooted in their unique social history in America, the difference is more one of function and experience than proof that one style is superior to another. In his reflection, he explores contemporary African- American Christian worship, beginning with an examination of the religious heritage African slaves brought with them to the new world. Next, he investigates the theology of African American worship, following with a focus on its characteristics and elements. He ends with a brief outline of some of the challenges facing Black worship.

## The African Religious Heritage

With many different African groups in America, they kept their religious groups as a source of their own identity. This is also known with other cultures. History has a way of changing things.

The Africans who came to America had a myriad of religious beliefs and practices, including the belief in a transcendent, benevolent God who created the universe and was its ultimate Provider[1] and though Europeans did not introduce the God of the Judeo-Christian ethic to Africans.[2]

Seemingly some problems have faced those contending that African religious beliefs and practices survived both the "Middle Passage" and the effects of slavery. One thought by E. Franklin Frazier, responded that slavery in the United States erased all the religious myths the slaves brought with them.[3] Others among them "stated by Melville Herskovits, argue that survivals, residuals, and "Africanisms" are still evident in African-American culture, especially its religious practices."[4] A balance between these two extremes are scholars like Albert J. Raboteau, admitted that the gods of Africa all but died in America indicating that early African -American religion was a syncretism of the African and the European. This school of thought contends that the African-American religion that remains to this day is a reworked Christianity crafted to meet the unique social context of the African American.[5]

An Africanism, for instance, that survived the "Middle Passage" and had a powerful impact on early African- American spirituality is the African understanding of life. Because Africans tend to view life holistically, the secular and the sacred are not mutually exclusive realities that exist in antagonistic tension but interconnected phenomena. Slaves held on to this understanding of life, and the result was that their worship was restricted to neither time nor place.

## A Theology of African-American Christian worship

People of African descent in North America tend to view life as a single system, their worship is integrative, holistic, and experiential. Historically, it has been woven into the being of their life.

Situations like born in slavery, weaned under Jim Crow segregation, and reared in discrimination, African American worship is linked with Black life. "The community is a grounding principle of Black Worship, understood by African-Americans as an encounter involving God, the worshiper, and the broader community."[6] For them worship is not primarily the expression of one's private devotion to God, but is rather a community event. This is the eschatological invasion of God into gathered community of victims empowering them with the divine Spirit from on high to keep on keeping on even though the odds might appear to be against them."[7] It is said that "Martin King, Jr. at its best Black worship is a social experience in which people from all walks of life affirm their unity and oneness in God."[8]

Always a divine experiment and dynamic happening, it is experienced as a response to the Holy Spirit's call to the believer to cast off his or her coat of cares and enter the divine presence. As God's presence is experienced anew, praise, adoration, thanksgiving, submission, and commitment are offered by the celebrant. "In African-American Christian worship God is known and understood as the One who sides with the weak and the oppressed. For Blacks, a God who does not care does not count, and they believe that the sovereign God continues to intervene in history in very concrete ways on their behalf. This God possesses absolute, unlimited power and delights in saving."[9]

God's Son, Jesus Christ, whose incarnational commitment to the poor was evidenced in His suffering, death, and resurrection, holds out hope for the personal and corporate transformation of humankind. There are no metaphysical distinctions between God and Jesus Christ in African-American Christian worship.

"Through the liberating presence of the Holy Spirit, both God the Father and God the Son are immediately present, and Blacks will fluctuate between calling upon

Jesus for strength to help them climb up "the rough side of the mountain "and testifying to an Almighty God about "how they got over."[10] African-American Christian worship is the corporate celebration of what God, through Jesus Christ, has done for the community in diaspora. In worship, celebrants confess their sins and accept God's forgiveness after they have been confronted by God, made uneasy by His judgments, and consoled by God's grace."[11]

For African Americans, worship is not as cerebral and rationalistic as it is experiential and dynamic. This is the case because African-American Christian worship focuses not so much on the transmission of abstract ideas and information as it does on the communal sharing of reality.[12] African Americans, in their worship, do not want only to learn something but to feel something, namely God's Spirit.[13] They aspire to know God personally rather than to know about God through doctrines and creeds, and they frown on the mere recitation of dogmas as proof that God is known. What matters most is to know God through God's revelation activities in their personal and corporate lives.[14] Yet their emphasis on experience does not mean that their worship is hollow and mere emotion. On the contrary, African-American worship has always, held emotion and intellect in creative tension, rejecting the either/or for the both/and paradigm.

## Characteristics of African-American Christian worship

**Pastoral Care.** Few things have provided African Americans with the coping and survival skills so vital to their experience in the United States as has worship. Black worship supplied slaves with effective psychological and emotional medicine to combat slavery's decimation of their sense of being and worth. Today it is still veritable the "Balm in Gilead" that keeps African

Americans sane and balanced in their world of traditionalized disenfranchisement and

powerlessness. In short, Black worship has always been about pastoral care, providing celebrants with comfort and healing. The question is how are comfort and healing engendered during worship? Comfort is experienced as worshipers sing

songs grounded in struggles that speak of a better tomorrow and hear testimonies from those who have "come over a way that with tears has been watered. "Comfort comes as prayer is offered that reminds celebrants of the power of God to right wrongs and preaches who know how to speak to aching hearts and confused minds expound the Word."[15] Yet it is drawing people into God's never-ending story of love that African-American worship functions best as pastoral care. As African Americans become aware of the fact that they have been integrated into God's story, their sense of being and wholeness is validated, as they respond by giving praise to God. **Liberation.** Another characteristic of African-American Christian worship is liberation African-American worship is a celebration of freedom in which people enter and experience the liberating presence of the Holy Spirit.

It has been called a "black happening, the time when the people gather together in the name of the One who promised that he would not leave ones alone in trouble."[16] A critical aspect of the liberation themes characteristic of Black worship is its refusal to be victimized by the tyranny of the clock. Liberation stemming from African-American Christian worship is also evident in the ways in which music is performed especially with Black singers and instrumentalists seldom being content to render a piece as it appears in print. Not so uncommon, they elect to search for notes and chords that strike a responsive in the African-American soul and experience. This brings me up to my next area.

**Empowerment.** African-American worship not only comforts and liberates but empowers for current and future struggles. Historically, the Black church has functioned as an agent of social cohesion, an agency of economic cooperation, a forum for political activity, and generally, as a haven in a hostile world."[17] Today, Black religious leaders continue to responsibly sensitize African Americans about the social, political, and religious structures that seek to steal not only them but all of God's people of their God given rights as persons. Worship leaders make sure that in worship people receive equipment and empowerment to comfort these structures and forces. "We truly worship as we are empowered by the Holy Spirit to embody Christ in and through us, "asserts Wilson Costen, who adds that in true and authentic worship there is a "dialectical relationship rather than a dichotomy between faith and practice, justice and ritual action (liturgy and justice), theological talk and doxological living, and sanctification and human liberation."[18]

**Celebration.** A fourth characteristic of African-American worship is celebration. Simply put, Black worship is a celebration of who God is, what God has done, is doing, and will do for His people. Such worship is celebratory because it is rooted in a "theology of thanksgiving honed on a peripheral jagged edge of life."[19] For a people still facing many challenges, waking up "clothed in your right mind and experiencing a measure of health and strength "is reason enough to praise God that things are as good as they are. In African-American worship people have a good time in the Lord, and it is not uncommon as they leave a service to hear them ask: "Didn't we have church today?!" Yet to have church is not just hand clapping, but to experience anew the liberating presence and power of Jesus Christ. By doing so with the Holy Spirit guiding you into the truth, you can never go wrong with whatever form of worship that is fitting for you.

## Elements of African-American Christian worship

Among the many elements of Black worship are prayer, music, and preaching. Together they form a combination for praise and thanksgiving.

**Prayer.** "In the African-American worship service, prayer is an irreplaceable that consists of three critical factors: the individual praying, the prayer itself, and the participation of the congregation."[20] The Spirit of God fully takes over the person who prays as much as He does the preacher, with the result that the person approaches "the throne of grace" humbly as an empty vessel waiting to be filled. Black prayer is not an escape mechanism, but "having a little talk with Jesus" and taking your burdens to the Lord." It is "approaching the throne of grace" on behalf of the community which continues to feel "like a motherless child" and is sure it is still "long ways from home." More than poetic posturing, this kind of prayer is rattlin' the gates of heaven" in the name of Jesus, who "sits high but bows low" and is "always on the main line" where He is ever "a-listenin' to hear somebody pray."

For many African Americans, they place a premium on the moment of prayer. For them this is the high point of the worship service. There is no problem for them to flock to the altar of prayer, firmly believing that there is additional flowing in the extra steps of faith. Whether they are at the altar or pew many will pray utterances of "yes, Lord," "Please God," and "Come, Holy Spirit." With other responses, African Americans are moved and involved in the prayer moment designed to create a sense that the burdens of life will be made lighter if they will not be removed altogether, and to offer strength for the journey ahead.

**Music.** "African- American spirituality, music plays second fiddle only to preaching in Black worship, with the two combining to create the minimum conditions for fulfilling, elevating worship service.[21] Wendell Mapson "indicated that the power of African-American worship is in the music, saying that the Blacks is in the music, saying that Blacks will forgive poor preaching if the worship service can be salvaged with good music.[22] During slavery days music was used to move the faithful to a predetermined spot for worship. "Slaves understood that music helped to create a feeling of freedom, facilitated an awareness of God's presence, and engendered an atmosphere in which God's grace could be experienced."[23]

Unlike the ancient Jews who refused to sing in a strange land (Psalm 137:1-4 NIV), slaves sang bequeathing to Western culture a genre of music that is uniquely and original American the Negro Spiritual. In the context of slavery, the meaning of the Spiritual was at once ambiguous and profound, transcendent and immanent, otherworldly and pertaining to this world. Thus, Spirituals protested the social conditions in which Blacks were the social conditions in which Blacks were locked even as they pointed to a better day of freedom and justice. Almost always, they communicated on several levels at once.

**Preaching.** Evidently there is little doubt that the African-American preacher occupies a prominent place in Black history. "Dating back to slavery, the African American preacher has been one with the capacity to "tell the story, "an ability grounded not so much in book knowledge as in an experience with Jesus Christ and an undeniable call to ministry."[24]

What is Black preaching? "Cleophus LaRue suggest or assumes that it is not so much a matter of style or technique as it is a function of the historical and contemporary experiences people of color have had in the United States out of which they forged a distinctive biblical hermeneutic. LaRue defines as characteristics of African-American preaching strong biblical content, creative use of language, appeal to emotions, and ministerial authorioty."[25] In a similar way, "Calvin B. Rock states that Black preaching is more a function of content than a form or rhetorical style, adding that it is the substance of Black preaching that informs and shapes its style."[26]

"The primary objective of African-American preaching is to enable the listener to experience the grace and love of Jesus Christ, the response to which is usually one of celebration and praise."[27] The cross of Christ is ever the substance and sum of Black preaching. It is told that the Seventh-Day Adventist preachers, the challenge to keep Christ as the core and center of their preaching is even more acute, given the premium Adventists place on content. Yet the author "Rock admonishes Black Adventist preachers to be true to both their cultural heritage believing that Black preaching and Seventh-day Adventist preaching are not mutually exclusive but complementary."[28]

African-American preaching is at its best when it is undergirded by two important hermeneutical principles. The first is that the gospel must be declared in the language of the people. The second is that the gospel must scratch where the people itch. As we look back historically, African-American preachers have had no problems about utilizing these two principles, especially the second. This is not to say that the Black sermon does not feed the mind as much as it satisfies the soul. However, it is in this regard that the genius of Black preaching is most evident. An African sermon is an experience of truth, not just a notion of truth. It must be felt, and not just heard. To be certain its cognitive elements must be present, but it must be so when it comes to the emotive realities. Black preaching is dialogical. It travels both vertically and horizontally. African-American preachers seldom, if ever, mount the pulpit if they have no word from the Lord, for this word is honed and sharpened by the preacher in his or her prayer chamber as well as in the preacher's study.

Black preachers know that each sermon they preach must originate with God, who will not bless the preaching moment if the preacher has not spent ample time with Him. In the pulpit, they carry an unending dialogue with God and the Congregation. "I feel the Spirit moving "is an utterance the African-American preacher will emit to let the people know that the preacher has established a connection with heaven and its hearing from God. "Help me, Holy Ghost "is a plea for divine help with the delivery of the sermon, to which the congregation may respond; Help him, Lord." A statement designed to bring the congregation into a preaching moment is "do I have a witness?" While, "tell it, preacher!" or "Preach!" testify that the preacher is on to something substantive.

Black preachers take evangelism seriously, they seldom just wind down, wrap up, and take their seats without appealing for people to accept and confess Jesus as Lord. When you fail to "open the doors of the church" is an unforgivable sin in the Black church, and it is known that the African-American preacher invite people to accept Christ at funeral services. Commonly known in the African American tradition is for people to accept Jesus is usually preceded and/or accompanied by a song. Tasks of African-American worship with no pretensions to being exhaustive, the following are some contemporary tasks of African-American worship. It must continue:

1.  To reflect the communal experience of African Americans without minimizing the ultimate focus of worship adoration of and of God!
2.  To hold in creative tension its unambiguous emphasis on correcting the injustices and inequities in this world with an eschatological focus on the life to come.
3.  To strike a balance between spontaneity and order.
4.  To be celebrative without succumbing to emotionalism.
5.  To liven up worship to celebrate Christ. African-American worship has played a vital role in the African-American community. Slaves who did not abandon their African religious heritage came to accept the God first in the "Invisible Institution" and later in their free churches. The reworked Christianity uniquely suited to meet the needs of their existential situation. Their celebration of God's redemptive acts in history and on their behalf, care, liberation, and empowerment. Most definitely, prayer, music, and the preached word are among the elements of their worship, destined to continue to be a "Balm in Gilead" for the journey ahead.

I want to focus on preaching specifically to the African American community, it says in Luke 4:18-19, (King James

Version) "The Spirit of the Lord is upon me, because he hath anointed me to preach the gospel to the poor; he hath sent me to heal the brokenhearted, to preach deliverance to the captives, and recovering of sight to the blind, to set at liberty them that are bruised. To preach the acceptable year of the Lord." These words will heal us.

# CHAPTER 3

## How Can I Apply Black Liberation Theology to the Apartheid practices in South Africa?

The first part of this chapter I will give a description of what Black Liberation Theology is. Secondly, I will indicate in this chapter what Black Liberation Theology means to me as a Black American living in the United States. The last two portions of this chapter, I will discuss the problems that still exist in South Africa concerning Apartheid practices and the need for Black Liberation Theology there. The last part of this chapter I will mention thought questions concerning the topic as a whole, also criticisms or comments of the authors on Black Liberation Theology and also authors from South Africa; and also, Apartheid practices in South Africa.

**Black Liberation Theology.** For a good starting point, Black Theology focuses upon the liberation of the oppressed. Blacks have been oppressed for years by Whites. There is a need for Black Theology both by Blacks and Whites to fully understand the struggles that Blacks are going through. Truly Blacks have suffered for centuries and suffering is still going on. The key word is suffering. How does the Western theology address suffering? It defines "the problem of suffering within the context of philosophical discourse, it inevitably locates the Christian approach to suffering in the wrong place. In philosophy, human suffering is an aspect of the problem of evil "Whatever else may be said about this philosophical definition of the problem of evil, the political action against evil is not built into it.

Thus, the problem is basically theoretical and not practical. Here then is one of the essential differences between the Bible and Greek philosophy. The latter tends to be more concerned about the theoretical formulation of the problem and less concerned about its practical elimination. The Bible is the exact reverse. Its emphasis is on what God has done in Jesus Christ and, the resurrection to destroy the powers of evil and give the oppressed the freedom to struggle against humiliation and suffering. The Bible has little or no interest in rational explanations regarding the origins of evil."[1]

I believe whole heartedly that God will deliver the Blacks from oppression if Blacks will believe this and stay faithful to (or in) God's service. As the Apostle Paul says in the 6th chapter of Ephesians "For our struggle is not against enemies of blood and flesh, but against the rulers, against the authorities, against the cosmic powers of this present darkness, against, the spiritual forces of evil in the heavenly places. Therefore, take up the whole armor of God, so that you may be able to withstand on that evil day and having done everything to stand firm." (Ephesians 6:12-13 New Revised Standard Version) These words quoted from Paul are not only for Blacks but for any race of people that is oppressed.

When one is the oppressor he(she) needs to be liberated from the power that dehumanizes himself or herself and any race or ethnic group. James Cone indicated that Western theology has been influenced more by philosophy than the Bible, that little attention has been addressed to the problem of suffering. Its focus has primarily been on the origins of evil, instead of the actual concerns of how the oppressed can and must act to destroy the social and political powers that perpetuate this evil. In my understanding of theology from my own horizon, I get this definition. Theology is a study or a science of religious doctrine, and also a study of God. If my definition is acceptable, then perhaps the Western theologians have taken heed to the first part of the definition. Philosophy is a science, and there is philosophy of religion. However, the latter part of my definition of theology is the study of God.

If the Western theologians really study God with a true sense of human dignity then there will be a change in their thinking of agape love. The problem is they rarely made agape love central in theology. They were unable to understand suffering and oppression. Apparently, the Western theologians missed the mark. That's why Black theology came on the scene. I know that it is hard sometimes for the Westerners to understand what oppression is when they haven't experienced it themselves. James Cone calls the Westerner in this case a spectator, and the oppressed the victims.

Cone goes on to say that Black people by their tradition came from Africa as slaves in this country. We have been mistreated. How does it feel when you can't drink from a public water fountain when you have been out in the hot sun all day? When the Black person becomes thirsty they come to a water fountain where it says, "For Whites Only." How does it feel when your bladder becomes full, and you must empty it as a black person, and find out that you must hold it until you get home, because the public rest rooms were for "Whites Only?" How does it feel when the White man takes your wife and sells her, and you will never see her again?

How does it feel when you are told to be a stud to impregnate other black women while pressured by a whip, when you know that the children of the women you got pregnant would be sold if they were healthy, and would be killed like an animal if they were unhealthy? And it hurts when you sweated in the fields and earned some property, and a stupid law comes into action where a white family takes your property? There must be an answer. The Blacks turned to the Bible. If God delivered the Israelites from the hands of the Egyptians, delivered Daniel from the Lion's Den, and the Hebrew children from the fiery furnace, he will deliver Black people from oppression. Our spiritual songs are a reflection of our suffering and oppression. I would like to share one of those songs which is a part of Black theology. The African folk song (Kum Ba Yah) meaning Come by Here/My Lord (Public Domain)

1. Come by here my Lord, Come by here, Come by here my Lord, Come by here, Come by here my Lord, Come by here, Oh Lord Come by here (Chorus)
2. Someone's singing Lord, Come by here, Someone's singing Lord, Come by here, Someone's singing Lord, Come by here, Oh Lord, Come by here
3. Someone's crying Lord, Come by here, Someone's crying Lord, Come by here, Someone's crying Lord, Come by here, Oh Lord, Come by here
4. Someone's dying Lord, Come by here, Someone's dying Lord, Come by here, Someone's dying Lord, Come by here, Oh Lord, Come by here

This song I thoroughly enjoy. Some of our ancestors have sung this song perhaps in the fields to keep their faith alive. I could imagine when our ancestors called for the Lord to come by their way as they begin to sing. While singing, someone was crying, because perhaps their child, their husband or their wife was taken away from them. While still singing, those who resisted their loved ones being taken away from them were brutally beaten and left to die. The ones still singing sang "someone is dying, Lord, come by here!" When I hear this song, I think about people as a whole not necessarily as a race of people. In a loving way, there are still some Whites who really want to experience our suffering because of their love for us. Surely, the impact of love and hate is in this country. However, Black Liberation Theology is a theology of hope to both Blacks and Whites. James Cone says, "We must probe our history, deep into its African roots, and ask about the relationship between the African shout and the Baptist moan, the River of Jordan in the spirituals and the river spirits of Western African religion. There should be no debate that we are African and not European."[2]

This substantiates the reflection on black spiritual songs. Years ago, I came across these words from Malcolm X. "What you and I need to do is to forget our differences. When we come together we don't come together as Baptists or Methodists. You don't catch hell because you're a Democrat or a Republican, you don't catch hell because you're a Mason or an Elk, and you sure don't catch hell because you're an American; because if you were an American, you wouldn't catch hell. You catch hell because you're a black man. You catch hell all of us catch hell, for the same reason." Malcolm's message is still true today. The mere fact that we are Black we need to unite with each other in our own struggles.

Tom Skinner, the author of "**How Black Is The Gospel?**", mentioned that "many Black Americans today bitterly denounce Christianity and the Bible because in their view, those who practice religious piety are among the leading exponents of hate, bigotry and prejudice. They feel that these "Bible-toting saints "perpetuate the most segregated hour of the week-eleven o'clock Sunday morning."[3] The statement by Skinner is still true today, however I must give some credit to the United Methodist Church and other denominations, they are trying to include all ethnic minority races in the Church, and also understand their cultural differences.

This is good, not saying that they have arrived, but it is a good start. Worshipping together with different ethnic backgrounds is a unique experience. The Church can be the answer if it is inclusive. In the midst of America's racial crisis, Christianity in its pure and true form alone can be the difference. The Black man, who has made noteworthy contributions to American life and culture in spite of oppression is in an ideal position to lead a spiritual crusade. The White man needs to swallow his pride and seek forgiveness for present crisis in America. The Black man, then, must forgive in a true demonstration of Christian love. If the White man will take the initiative, he will find a cooperative response. Neither action will be more than skin deep unless Christ Himself is in control. If you want to change a man truly, you must change him from inside out. You can't really change him by just shifting his environment. One's heart must be changed as we receive peace laid down by God.

## "Black Liberation Theology/Its Meaning to Me as a Black American Living in the U.S.A."

Black liberation theology speaks specifically to the conditions of blacks in America. I am black so therefore it speaks to me. I can remember back in the 1960's there was an idea that God was dead. I said to myself, this cannot be true. I need a God who is alive and can be powerful enough to change the hearts of men and women to love each other instead of exemplifying hate and malice toward others. I saw so much racial prejudice amongst Blacks and Whites in the 1960's. I was there in Detroit Michigan in 1965 when the late Rev. Dr. Martin Luther King, Jr. marched for the hope of freedom for all. Little did I know that 2 years later in the same city Detroit, a riot would break out where many people were hurt and killed. There was no demonstration of real love. I said to myself, "perhaps God is dead." In 1968, I entered the United States Navy in San Diego, California. Believe it or not, but it is true, the same day that the Rev. Dr. Martin Luther King, Jr. was assassinated there was an earthquake in San Diego. The Sailors felt the tremor and were frightened. When the Black sailors heard the news of King's assassination, fights broke out everywhere. In a small voice I replied, "God are you there?"

Perhaps the theological concept that "God is Dead" in the 1960's really shook people up. So much racial violence and hatred. In a way, I was glad that the 60's were over. There must be a different story for the 1970's. A new theology was introduced in the 70's. The theology was, Black Theology. The concept of "God is Dead" in the 60's is gone. In the 70's, God is not Dead, "He is Black", is the theology. I was told that this Black theology specifies that God is the God of the oppressed and Christ's gospel is the gospel of liberation. Blacks for years have been considered oppressed. This whole concept of racial prejudice amongst Blacks and Whites of the Old Testament story of how the Egyptians were the oppressor and the Israelites were the oppressed. God helped out the Israelites, and I feel the same about Blacks in America. He will help us too!

Most of my life when I was in school, I had White teachers who told me that I would never amount to anything. That was a racial remark, and I resented that statement bitterly. Wrestling with my own frustrations I used whiteners trying to change my skin color to be accepted by Whites. That was stupid of me to do that, but I did. I even treated my own race bad, because I hated the thought of being Black, to go through life this way. I'm glad that Black theology came on the scene, because I began to believe in myself and my blackness. I'm proud of my Blackness, because God made me Black. God does not make junk. I am somebody, a slogan that Rev. Jesse Jackson uses is so meaningful to me and others. The late singer James Brown made a song entitled, "Say It Loud, I'm Black and I'm Proud", also helped out the Blacks to be aware of Blackness and their identity. As a Black American living in America, I find it very hard at times to relate to Whites particularly when racism still exists.

However, in my heart as a Christian, I am concerned about White brothers and sisters repenting. In terms of conversion I will leave that up entirely to the Holy Spirit. I'm not going to get uptight about White people not being converted. My main concerns are first of all that I have my heart right with God. I pray that Whites will also. If not, then perhaps Black theology can be a threat or challenge for their conversion Sadly, a type of "conversion" is preached which leaves racism in tact in the White churches. In all of my biblical and theological training, I have been taught to focus upon the gospel. I think it is very important to know about the teachings of Jesus and the Apostles (which is the gospel.)

After reading over various works on Black theology by Cone, Skinner, Bruce, Jones, and Boesak, I am even more convinced that the implications of the gospel are found in Black theology. The gospel always turns people off. Whenever the truth touches us, we feel threatened. When Jesus told the truth to the Pharisees and the Sadducees, they felt threatened. We feel the same way today sometimes when the gospel speaks to us. When the gospel message tells us to turn the other cheek when we are hit. How far must the Blacks turn their cheeks when we have been mistreated for years? As a Christian, I'm sure we can answer that! The gospel challenges our comfort zones. It confronts us at the heart of our stability. When we are challenged by our comfort zones, that means that we must come out of our comfort zones. The comfort zones may be our economics, social, whiteness, and blackness. When our comfort zones come before God it makes us little gods or idol gods. We must get rid of our gods in order to be free in relation to Christ. The gospel will shake up our inner most being whether we are black or white. I thank God for my Christian background. I believe that in order to become a Christian you must die to the world and become new in Christ, and that's what baptism is: the sign or sacrament by which we are accepted into the Church.

Of course, there are a lot of people who have been baptized who don't become new people. You can dip the Devil under water. When the Devil comes up out of the water, he's still the Devil, because the Devil's heart hasn't changed. When you are baptized, your heart should change for a new birth experience. Some of your White churches have been talking about love, but yet that love is void. As a Black American living in this country, I would address the Whites in this fashion. I think the White's concept of love should be revolutionized. For many of us, love means allowing the neighbor to do anything he or she wants and not trying to protect oneself.

Love in most churches has practiced some kind of passive response that the sufferer makes when he or she is oppressed. Love must be revolutionized to the point where people are not permitted to talk about love unless they also talk about power and justice. Love without power and justice is not Christian love. Black theology does not encourage Black people to hate White people, but it encourages Black love for White people. Love sometimes does not describe what our needs are. I love my wife, my children, grandchildren, parents, brothers, sisters, and a lot of other people. I do love everybody; however, I do not love them in the same way, but I still love them. In a black/white context, love means to me that I must be friendly first of all. I must try to understand my White brother and sister, and they in turn must understand me. We must communicate to make this development of our relationship to grow. If my White counterparts are the oppressors, I must stop this oppression by love and not hate. Hate really never stops oppression, it only creates more wounds and more oppression. Some of my people who are Black have stated that the only good oppressor is a dead oppressor. That statement is just as bad as a White person saying, "the only good Indian is a dead Indian!" Both statements are non-Christlike I don't think that we can solve any problem by wishing that people have to be dead in order to be good. God is good, and if we work at it hard enough, we can be good also by his grace. Perhaps if we get so close to God, the further we turn from Him, because of the Devil.

Some of your Black Christian ethicists may say "that if that is the only way that oppression must stop by one being dead perhaps that can be an act of love!" I don't think that killing someone regardless of their color could be the act of love. It's absurd to kill all Whites, the oppressors, and let all the Blacks live, the oppressed. However, there is more of a deep theological problem going on. You can kill people not only physically, you can kill them psychologically, socially, and reduce them to non-human beings by the way you relate to them. When some of my White teachers earlier in my life told me that I would never amount to anything, I felt angry and hurt. If I took their advice it would have killed me psychologically, emotionally, socially, and spiritually.

All of this would have reduced me to nothing. Thanks be to God that I didn't take them seriously. I was stubborn enough in Christ to make their statement wrong. I know that some White Americans have attempted to kill Black people socially, politically and theologically. Some White theologians have used this statement to keep Blacks in line: Obey your Master, serve your Master at all costs. Wait just a minute! How can you obey your Master that is disobedient to

God by dehumanizing you? How can you obey your Master when your Master has taken your land, your children, your wives, and others? That kind of obedience is suicidal, its ignorant. We still have some Uncle Toms saying "yes Master" My only Master is my Lord and Savior Jesus Christ. He is the only Master that I will totally obey. Of course, I will give unto Caesar what is Caesar's, and I will give to God what is God's, because the Lord told us to. Now of course some of the Whites may disagree with some of my comments, they have their rights to do so.

Of course, in every structure in which White people participate they have the last word. If that is the case that is White racism. If the Black people have the last word and haven't truly understood the Whites, then that's Black racism. We need to keep Black theology as our hope. As soon as we turn our backs from Black theology it will give Whites the continued upper hand. Whites have stated, keep the Blacks in their place. If there is continued racism, then of course all of us should keep ourselves in our place with God being our helper. Our place should be God's place. We are under no one yet, because all of us have freedom in Christ. Our Father directs all.

## Apartheid Practices in South Africa/The Need for Black Liberation Theology

After the National Party gained power in South Africa in 1948, its all- white government immediately began enforcing existing policies of racial segregation under a system of legislation called apartheid. Apartheid, (Afrikaans: "Apartness") policy that governed relations between South Africa's white minority and white majority and sanctioned racial segregation and political and economic discrimination against non-whites. Apartheid in South

Africa reigned from 1948 and still lives on today because of racism in that country. Released from prison in 1990, Nelson Mandella participated in the eradication of apartheid and in 1994 became the first Black president in South Africa, forming a multiethnic government to oversee the country's transition. However, Apartheid practices still exist. I have discussed racial prejudice here in America amongst the whites and the blacks and the need for Black theology in America. Racial prejudice exists everywhere, but one main country that perpetuate racism is the country of South Africa.

(This article was produced for South African History Online on 05-Jul-2012) in 1985 the South African government has enacted a law where What is it like to be or live under Apartheid? Apartheid destroys land rights Eighty-four percent of South Africans are forced to live on 13 per cent of the land because they are Black. Black communities are bulldozed to make room for Whites. Millions of blacks have been moved from white areas by force. Apartheid destroys black family life. Laws prevent husbands and wives from living together in white-only cities. However, in 1985 the South African government has enacted a law where white people can marry blacks and also have sexual intercourse with them.

Women who find work as maids feed white children while their own go hungry in the barren "homelands" often hundreds of miles away. Consequently, husbands and wives visit weekly or monthly if they live in the same area, otherwise they visit once or twice a year with each other and their children. Apartheid starves blacks to death in rural areas. One of every five rural black babies die before their first birthday, many from lack of food while South Africa exports $2 billion worth of food a year. That's tragic! Apartheid denies decent wages. Africans earn on the average less than a third what white workers do. Over 60 percent of urban blacks live below the established poverty level. Apartheid denies access to education.

Whites receive a free education, while blacks must pay for their children to go to school. The Apartheid government defends white wealthy by force. It jails exiles and kills those who protest against apartheid. It attacks neighboring countries which support South African freedom fighters. The question is, "what we can do here in America as consumers is to protest the apartheid practices going on in South Africa?") Don't buy products made in South Africa. Ask your bank or neighborhood coin shop to stop selling Kruggerands and other products of South Africa such as wine. Write your state legislators and ask them to support legislation which would take away any investments that the states may have in this country and its companies which operate in South Africa. This would be a real threat to South Africa if the U.S. A. could do this. I don't think the companies here in America would be willing to do that.

Write your congressional representatives and senators and ask them to support economic sanctions against South Africa until it ends the system of apartheid. I don't know if this is the answer, but at least it's a start. The information thus far on the apartheid practices may be googled from the "**Ohio Coalition Against Apartheid.**" **Duration 1984-unknown existed in the late 1980's and may have continued until 1994.** Allen Boesak, the author of, "Apartheid Is a Heresy", stated the following words, "we should assume a more active role in the struggle against racism.

A. A black thinker and activist W.E.B. Dubois has been proved absolutely correct in his assertion that one of the central problems of the twentieth century is the race problem.

B. Instead of abating, racism has grown. Christians in Western Europe have become increasingly aware of the problem there, and in the United States racism in numerous ways, has once more taken on a cloak of respectability.

C. Racism has taken on new, more subtle forms, and has found powerful allies in such ideologies as militarism, nationalism, and national security.

D. In the political field, it seems as if liberal politics has come to the end of its solution and its energy. The responsibility of the Church in such a situation is now greater than ever before, not only to challenge the myopic theologized patriotism of yet another brand of evangelicalism; but to proclaim the vision of the Kingdom of God, transcending the narrow boundaries of race and nationalism and bringing justice to the poor and the oppressed.

E.  The last reason lies in the reality of the situation of the government of South Africa itself. Not only is South Africa the most blatantly racist country, but also the country where the Church is most openly identified with the racism and oppression that exist in that society."[4]

If the Church and the government is identified with racism in South Africa this creates a problem. Any country that blatantly practices racism is sinful and need a change in that system. Government and Church racism is called, "institutionalized racism." Where there is institutionalized racism, there is no chance for the Blacks to survive and live a productive life, unless the South African government and Church will make a change. Racism is a sin because the New Testament affirms the principle of equality and actual differentiation of all people and nations, each with its own right of existence, as well as the unity of the entire human family, and because the commandment to love one's neighbor also manifests itself in justice. "The Methodist Church of South Africa affirms that apartheid is the negation of:

1.  The dignity with which God has endowed man in creating him in his own image;
2.  The work of Jesus Christ through his coming into the world to live, die and rise for mankind, thus freeing it from bondage for fullness of life;
3.  The reconciliation effected by Christ between man and God, and man and man.

Apartheid is simply a socio-political policy, but sinful contradiction of the Gospel which cannot be justified on biblical or theological grounds and is therefore, an ideology, which the Methodist Church rejects as heresy."[5] If Black theology is continued in South Africa it could help alleviate the apartheid practices there. However, other theologians and authors may have another view. The African theologians view "Black theology as a judgment on White Christianity in South Africa. At its deepest it is not a reaction against the living out of this message by Whites. Black theology was a painful reminder that we have been unable to give these Black people the Christ of the Bible, because they cannot see this Christ in their lives."[6]

To comment on this quote about Black theology as a painful reminder of Christ in the Bible whereas this Christ was not seen in their lives. I must say that Black theology can and will open up awareness to both the whites and the blacks. Painful it may be, but I also say that Black theology tells the truth. Whenever the truth is told it may attack us where our wrongs are. There is nothing right about apartheid practices in South Africa, or anywhere. The South African government and the Dutch Reformed Churches of South Africa need to hear what Black theology is talking about. Perhaps some Black theologians in Africa do not understand our Black theology in America. Some people still feel that Black theology is employed as an aid in establishing and expanding Black power. This concept about Black theology is false. Black theology calls the attention of both Blacks and Whites to wrongs in terms of racial prejudice. Our wrongs can be reverted to right if Christ is our guide. We are known to label people in categories such as if you are poor you are generally nothing.

If you are rich you are everything. We need to come away from labeling and get right with God. The father of Black theology in South Africa is Basil Moore. His essays have communistic influence. Truly the Marxist view is the form of liberation, but that's not God's way of liberating us. The Marxist view is that man is primarily the product of his social environment. The

Christian response is to spread the gospel everywhere and live out the gospel. Some of the Christians haven't done this, so therefore other theologies have come into existence. There must be a continuous dialogue amongst all types of theologies to get a better understanding. Marx had no doctrine of sin; he saw alienation in purely material terms. The African theologian would address a different kind of an approach to theology because of an African experience.

On the other hand, the Black theologians in America would use Black theology because of their experience here in America. Desmond Tutu, the leading South African theologian, and the Bishop quoted these words: "Black theology is more thoroughly and explicitly political than African theology is. We cannot be lulled into complacency by a doctrine of pie in the sky which is a reprehensible travesty of the gospel of the Incarnation. It has an existential urgency which African theology has so far appeared to lack. African theology has tended to be more placid; to be interested still too much with what I call anthropological concerns. This has been its most important achievement in the quest for indigenization."[7] Desmond Tutu indicated that the African theology fails when it comes to addressing contemporary problems of the modern African. Desmond Tutu admitted that Black theologians or Black theology can give the African theologians some lessons in the area of contemporary problems of Blacks.

Desmond Tutu mentioned that African theology has become too serene and peaceful to mankind and its concerns. I clearly hear Tutu's message. It's good to study mankind and its concerns which is anthropology, but what are you going to do about the concerns of mankind? Bishop Tutu had his problems of injustice towards Blacks in South Africa. Bishop Tutu was born near a small town, west of Johannesburg. When he grew up he witnessed racial prejudice coming from the Whites of South Africa. Bishop Tutu studied to be a doctor, but he had to drop out of school because his father couldn't afford the expenses. He went on into teaching but later he quit because the South African government enacted a system of inferior education toward Blacks.

After all of this had occurred in his life, Bishop Tutu entered the ministry. He completed his training at one of the colleges in Johannesburg. He left the country to receive his other degrees in England. With his accomplishments later on he became a Bishop of the Anglican Church and also the Nobel Peace Prize recipient of 1984. Bishop Tutu criticizes the apartheid practices in South Africa, and he also wants withdrawal of investments of outsiders to do business with South Africa, as I discussed this earlier in the chapter. Praise be to Almighty God, Bishop Tutu donated all of the $192,000.00 of the Nobel Peace Prize Award to South African youths for an educational scholarship fund. Bishop Tutu hears the call for Black theology in South Africa.

Readily so, whenever racism or inequality is expressed there is a need for Black theology whether it's in America, South Africa or anywhere. Let us understand this theology.

**My Comments:** I will discuss what I have talked about thus far in this chapter. Secondly, I will formulate thought Questions concerning the topic as a whole. Finally, I will have comments or criticisms of the authors on Black Liberation theology and also Apartheid practices in South

Africa. I used James Cone's definition of Black Liberation theology coming from his book entitled, "God of the Oppressed." Cone gave a definition of the Western theological implications which derives from Greek philosophy. Greek philosophy is good to know, but it's not good to use its concepts on a race to dehumanize them. Black theology is very much needed for liberation. Black theology focuses upon the Bible and its emphasis to destroy the powers of evil. Greek philosophy is primarily concerned about its practical elimination of evil is by knowledge which is good.

The author, Tom Skinner who wrote, "How Black Is The Gospel", mentioned that many Black Americans today denounce Christianity because of the so called White Christians practicing racial prejudice and segregation. Later on, in Tom Skinner's book, he talked about a new voice of Black evangelism posing himself. Skinner says that the gospel of Jesus Christ is relevant to the black man's condition, relevant in liberating him, and his white brother, and in teaching him to fight against injustice. If blacks and whites are to be reconciled, he states, we must all give ourselves up to Jesus Christ the radical. To reiterate my feelings on Black Theology, my primary concerns are:

1. Black theology specifies God is the God of the oppressed.
2. Black theology reflects back to the Bible and reminds us how many groups were oppressed by the oppressor.
3. Black Theology brought on belief in myself, and my blackness.
4. Black theology challenges white oppressors to repent.
5. Black theology keeps my heart right with God.
6. Black theology focuses me to the gospel.
7. Black theology encourages black love for white people.

The apartheid practices in South Africa is sinful, both the Black theologians in America, and the African theologians in Africa are aware of this. To sum up the problems of Apartheid practices in South Africa, I can use one word, that word is <u>inhuman</u>. Do the South African racists have a heart, can they be revolutionized like some of the Whites in America who have been introduced to Black theology? When we read articles and books on apartheid practices in South Africa, your stomach churns. How does it feel if you were living in South Africa as a Black living in a cell not a home without running water or electricity? Most of these homes may have more than eight people living under those conditions. There is a question that I may ask. Can some of these Blacks relocate? Perhaps not, because the apartheid system keeps them where they are. They are forced to stay where they are and live where the conditions are deplorable.

The Christian answer to this problem would be to strongly proclaim that the Church exists not to separate people, nor to acquiesce in the deliberate disruption of families and communities, but to build fellowship. I sometimes wonder if we can preach the gospel without regard to this critical problem of relocation under apartheid. Every person on earth should have a chance of their particular choices. No matter what translation the Bible contains several accounts of illustrations of the worth of an individual. The three examples that I want to share are: the shepherd's concern for the lost sheep (Luke 15:1-7); God's sending of Elijah to rebuke the king (1 King 18:16-19) or Nathan to scold David (2 Samuel 12:1-7) Evil in itself can involve the whole family or society. The society of South Africa needs to change. How long will Black Africans in South Africa have to suffer? No one really knows that answer but God.

I mentioned earlier in this chapter that Bishop Tutu hears the call for Black theology in South Africa. I pray that some of our Black Christians here in America that have a strong hold on Black theology will travel if they can to South Africa with a strong force exemplifying what Black theology is. Perhaps if more Blacks from all portions of the continent center their attention on South Africa and its apartheid practices something could be done about the situation there. As of today, apartheid practices stopped for over 20 years, or did they under Nelson Mandella's presidency.

What's happening now is the current apartheid practices in South Africa such as:

- University standards are dropping
- Global competition is in decline
- South Africa holds the most unequal society in the world
- The pay gap one of the worst in the world
- Trade Unions out of control
- Government corruption is an epidemic problem
- Violent crime
- HIV/AIDS epidemic amongst highest in the world

The African National Congress led by Jacob Zuma is criticized because the power is dominated by members of this party. Is this apartheid in reverse? Any form of apartheid is sinful. Everybody has ideas to solve a problem, but we do not know which one of our ideas will work unless we try them. We must do something. That something is, try God! In the book entitled, "Irruption of The Third World", by Virginia Fabella and Sergio Torres, you will find these words quoted for apartheid practices in South Africa before their freedom in 1994. "This situation has brought about not only untold suffering and constriction of every aspect of the people's life- economic, political, cultural, racial, religious, spiritual- but also untimely death to children, men, and women by the millions. Poverty dehumanizes not only the countless poor, but also the rich in that they benefit from the suffering of countless others and grow insensitive to the claims of life."[8]

I wish the last part of the preceding sentence about the rich being insensitive to the poor and their conditions of suffering would apply to the whites in South Africa. I pray that they did make a change. As I close out this chapter I would like to interject some thought questions for the reader, and also for myself to reflect upon.

1. Is it true that most people think that Tom Skinner is a very radical Black theologian? As a whole yes, but Tom Skinner is saying the same thing about Black theology as James Cone does. The difference of the two Black theologians is that James Cone is milder in his approach to the use of Black theology.

2. When most Americans, whether they are Black or White read African theology, they have mixed emotions about historical data of Africans. We sometimes say to ourselves how absurd it is the way the African culture is. The Africans could say the same thing about America's complexed culture.

3.  The existing structure of the Church cannot be redeemed. It has to be destroyed. If there is continued racial prejudice going on, then the existing structure of the Church should be destroyed.

4.  Have the blacks ever accepted the laws of the society? I don't think so. Their obedience to the laws if they are unjust sets a dead spirit in their hearts.

5.  Is it true that women in the Women's Liberation Movement use some of the very same expressions of Black theology such as self- definition for example? I'm in agreement with this statement.

6.  Would you say that Christ is to be found at work, almost exclusively where there is suffering or oppression? I would answer yes. God is everywhere whether there is suffering or not. God is tired of people being exploited or mistreated. God works in mysterious ways. God has touched the hearts of many to focus their attention on the blacks in South Africa and also the starving blacks in Ethiopia. The Church is militant right now, because of its sins of fighting against God. However, the Church will be triumphant when Christ returns and get his Bride.

7.  The affliction of the South African blacks is truly evil. The scripture says, "All the days of the afflicted are evil: but he that is of a merry heart hath a continual feast." Proverbs 15:15 (King James Version) In order to get along with one another we need to have happy hearts. I am reminded that God is the Lord and ruler of our lives so let's continue to love one another, because a broken spirit dries our bones, and envy rotten our bones.

# CHAPTER 4

## Oppression of African Americans/ The Willie Lynch Letter and The Making of a Slave

For the purpose of this chapter, I will not use derogatory words that Willie Lynch used to degrade African American slaves. My reference can be found on the internet, www.lojsociety.org Let's Make a Slave. In the Introduction the infamous "Willie Lynch" letter gives both African and Caucasian students and teachers some insight, concerning the brutal and inhumane psychology behind the African slave trade which was morally wrong. The materialistic viewpoint of Southern plantation owners that slavery was a "business" and the victims of chattel slavery were merely pawns in an economic gain of debauchery, crossbreeding, interracial rape, and mental conditioning of a Negroid race, they considered subhuman.

There were both moral arguments and legal positions to the question of slavery in the South. On one side, it began with the "Rights of Man", and descended to sticking for it to have a decent appearance on the statute book. On the other side, it began with the uplifting of the heathen; and descended to a denial of the applicability of moral principles to the question; said Holland of North Carolina, "It is admitted that the condition of slaves in the Southern states is much superior to those in Africa." (Holland's opinion) Who then will say that trade is immoral? But in fact, morality has nothing to do with this traffic, for Joseph Clay declared, "it must appear that every man of common sense, that the question could be considered in a commercial point of view only."

The other side declared that, "by laws of God and man these capture Negroes, are entitled to their freedom as clearly and as absolutely as we are. The moral questions were argued back and forth, but there was no question of the tremendous profitability using slavery in exchange for molasses, sugar, textiles, and massive free labor of the cotton production on numerous plantations in the South. The system began with a conspiratorial battle of wits between the European traders and African chiefs. Slave traders were required to know not only the state of the trade, if they were to "see a profit," but also know the likely supply of ships on the other. Also, the varying of many different standards of payment. Coins were seldom or never used on the coast.

Mostly the chiefs and slave traders dealt in rolls of tobacco, barrels of rum, and firearms and generally in lengths of iron or copper, or in pots and basins of brass. The slaver's books are full of all of this. The African slave trade, and the tedious burden placed on the backs of African people, most will agree that the psychological damage, and atrocities inflicted on Black people during that point of time, and even today, are the most outrageous examples of injustice and depression ever experienced by humanity. The William Lynch speech was delivered on the bank of the James River in 1712. His speech or message is still true today. Here are some of the things that he said, "While Rome used cords of wood for crosses for standing human bodies along its old highways in great numbers, you are here using a tree and rope on occasion.

I caught the whiff of dead slaves hanging from a tree a couple of miles back. You are not only losing valuable stocks by hangings, you are having uprisings, slaves are running away, your crops are sometimes left in the fields too long for maximum profit, you suffer occasional fires and your animals are killed. Gentlemen, you know what problems are; I do not need to elaborate. I am not here to enumerate your problems; however, I am here to introduce you to a method of solving them." Willie Lynch had a bag before him. In that bag he had a fool proof method for controlling Black slaves. He guaranteed that if the method was installed correctly, it will control the slaves for at least 300 years. He said that his method was simple, and any member of their family or overseer could use it. I am not going to list all of the methods, but enough to get an understanding about Willie Lynch tactics.

In his tactics he indicated that distrust is stronger than trust, and envy is stronger than adulation, respect, or admiration. When the Black slaves received this indoctrination, this response will become self-refueling and self-generation for hundreds of years, maybe thousands.

**# 1 Principle**- You must pitch the old Black male verses the young Black male, and the young Black male against the old Black male. You must use the Dark skin slaves verses the Light skin slaves, and the Light skin slaves verses the Dark skin slaves. You must use the Female verses the Male, and the Male verses the Female. You must also have your White servants and overseers distrust all Blacks, but it is necessary that your slaves trust and depend on us. <u>They must love, respect, and trust only us.</u> Gentlemen, these kits are the keys to control. Use them. Have your wives and children use them, never miss an opportunity. If used intensively for one year, the slaves themselves will remain perpetually distrustful.

Willie Lynch used a technique of division of the slaves by having the oldest Black men against the youngest Black men. He used the Dark skin slaves against the Light skin slaves. He used the Females against the Males, and the Males against the Females. He used tactics of power for White servants and overseers to control the slaves. Frederick Douglas stated these words "Conscious of the injustice and wrong that they were every hour perpetrating and knowing what they themselves would do were they victims of such wrongs, they were constantly looking for the first signs of dread retribution. They watched therefore, with skilled and practiced eyes, and learned to read with great accuracy, the state of mind and heart of the slave, through his stable face. Unusual sobriety, apparent abstraction, sullenness and indifference- indeed any mood out of the common way afforded ground for suspicion and inquiry."

Let us make a slave what do I need? First of all, we need a Black negro man, a pregnant Negro woman and her baby Negro boy. Second, I will use the same basic principles in breaking a horse, combined with some more sustaining factors.

## # 2 Principle

1. Both horse and negro are no good to the economy in the wild or natural state.
2. Both must be broken and tied together for orderly production.
3. For the orderly futures, special and particular attention must be paid to the female and the young offspring.
4. Both must be crossbred to produce a variety and division of labor.
5. Both must be taught to respond to a particular new language.
6. Psychological and physical instruction containment must be created for both. Note: Neither principle alone will suffice for good economics.

All principles must be employed for the orderly good of a nation. Accordingly, both a wild horse and a wild or natural Negro is dangerous even if captured for they will have a tendency to seek their customary freedom, and in doing so, might kill you in your sleep. You cannot rest. They sleep while you are awake and are awake while you are asleep. They are dangerous near the family house and it requires too much labor to watch them away from the house. Above all you cannot get them to work in a natural state. Hence, both the horse and the negro must be broken that is to break them from one form of mental life to another – keep the body and take the mind. In other words, break the will to resist. Now the breaking process is the same for both the horse and the negro, only slightly varying in degrees.

For economic planning you must keep your eye and thoughts on the female and the offspring of the horse and the Negro. Pay little attention to the generation of original breaking but concentrate on future generations. Therefore, if you break the female mother, she will break the offspring in its early years of development and, when the offspring ids old enough to work, she will deliver it up you for her normal female productive tendencies will have been lost in the original breaking process. With two Negro males in the natural state a pregnant Negro woman with her infant offspring. Take the stud horse, break him for limited containment. Completely break the female horse until she becomes very gentle whereas you or anybody can ride her in comfort.

Bred the mare and the stud until you have the desired offspring. Then you can turn the stud to freedom until you need him again. Train the female horse whereby she will eat out of your hand, and she will turn and train the infant horse to eat out of your hand also. When it comes to break the uncivilized Negro, use the same process, but vary in degree and step up the pressure so as to do a complete reversal of the mind.

**# 3 Principle**- Take the meanest and most restless Negro, strip him of his clothes in front of the remaining Negroes, the female, the Negro infant, tar and feather him, tie each leg to a different horse in opposite directions, set him on hire and beat both horses to pull him apart in front of the remaining Negroes. The next step is to take a bullwhip and beat the remaining Negro male to the point of death in from of the female and the infant. Don't kill him, but put the fear of God in him, for he can be useful for future breeding. (This is pure torture)

**#4 Principle**- Take the female and run a series of tests on her to see if she will submit to your desire willingly. Test her in every way because she is the most important factor food good economics. If she shows any sign of resistance in submitting completely to your will, do not hesitate to use the bullwhip on her to extract the last bit of something out of her. Take care not to kill her, for in doing so, you spoil economics. When in complete submission, she will train her offspring in the early years to submit to labor when they become of age. The breaking process of the female Negro, we have reversed relationships. In her natural uncivilized state, she would have a limited protective tendency toward her independent male offspring and would raise the female offspring to be dependent like her. Nature had provided time with this balance.

We reversed nature by burning and pulling one civilized negro apart and bullwhipping the other to the point of death-all in her presence. By her being left alone, unprotected, with the male image destroyed, the ordeal caused her to move from her psychological dependent state. To a frozen independent state of independence, she will raise her male and female offspring in reversed roles. For fear of the young man's life, she will psychologically train him to be mentally weak and dependent but physically strong. Because she has become psychologically independent. What have you got? You've got a Negro woman out front and the man behind and scared. This is a perfect situation for sound sleep and economics.

Before the breaking process, we had to alertly be on guard at all times. Now we can sleep soundly, for out of frozen fear, this woman stands guard for us. He cannot get pass her infant slave process. **He Is A Good Tool, Now Ready To Be Tied To The Horse At A Tender Age.** By the time a Negro boy reaches the age of sixteen, he is soundly broken in and ready for life's sound and efficient work and the reproduction of a unit of a good labor force.

**There is a Food for the Thought** from the Internet www.lojsociety.org/Let's Make a Slave

Dear Black Americans: This is our open letter of thanks. We will always be in debt to you for your labor. You built this country and were responsible for the great wealth we still enjoy today. Upon your backs, laden with stripes we sometimes had to apply for disciplinary reasons, you carried our nation. We thank you for your diligence and your tenacity. Even when we refuse to allow you to even walk in our shadows, you followed close behind believing that someday we would accept you and treat you like men and women. We publicly acknowledge Black people for raising our children, attending to our sick, preparing our meals while we were occupied with the trappings of the good life.

Even when the time when we found pleasure in your women and enjoyment in seeing your men lynched, maimed, burned, some of you continued to watch over us and our belongings. We simply cannot thank you enough. Your bravery on the battlefield, despite being classified as three-fifths of a man was and still is outstanding. Now that we control at least 90 percent of all the resources and wealth of this nation, we have Black people to thank the most. We can only think of these sacrifices you and your families made to make it all possible. You were there when it all began, and you are still with us today, protecting us from those Black people who have the temerity to speak against or pass transgressions. For all your labor, which created our wealth, for your resisting the message of trouble making Blacks like Washington, Delany, Garvey, Bethune, Tubman, and Truth, for fighting and dying on our battlefields, we thank you. Perhaps we have moved away from William Lynch techniques but have we. Some systems take a very long time to change.

The year 2017 brings on a lot of frustrated moments not only for Blacks but also Whites. Crime rates have increased such as White police officers killing Black men, and Black women. In addition to that Black men killing White men and White police officers. There are so many Black lives taken by Whites. This reaction in 2017 brings on a movement called, "Black Lives Matter." Yes, Black lives matter. We have struggled so hard to get where we are now here in 2017. We talk about so many Black lives taken. We are still killing ourselves more so than White people killing us. It is interesting that the homicide rate in New York is below the national average. The city of Chicago has more murders accounted for than New York and Los Angeles combined as shared in the article called **"The Economist June 29, 2017."**

I am saddened that Blacks represent 13% of America's population, yet in 2015 they represented 52% of the slain. The period between 1980 and 2013, 262,000 Black men were murdered

in America, that's more than four times America's total number
of casualties in Viet Nam. All of these murders come from the
combination of poverty, family instability, epidemics of drug use,
and Black lives are valued less. The city of Baltimore Maryland
is in the shambles more homicides than ever, such as over 200
homicides in 1980 up to over 400 homicides in 2017 thus far. That
is alarming! Covering a period from January to May. We need
Jesus in our lives to stamp out all of the violence and stupendous
things that we do. Jesus is our Savior. He can fix anything that is
broken. In our brokenness we can never be great until we find **True
Greatness**. The Word says, "[1]At that time the disciples came to
Jesus and asked, "Who is the greatest in the kingdom of heaven?"
[2] He called a child whom he put among them, [3] and said, "Truly
I tell you, unless you change and become like children, you will
never enter the kingdom of heaven. [4] Whoever becomes humble
like this child is the greatest in the kingdom of heaven. [5] Whoever
welcomes one such child in my name welcomes me. Matthew 18:1-5
(New Revised Standard Version). Generations after generations
we fight the same battle of nothing less because we are not real.
What I am saying is that we are afraid to face reality. We talk about
integration but are we integrated? We talk about unity, but are we
unified? We talk about justice, but are we justified? We talk about
our comfort zones, but are we afraid to get out of them? The Civil
Rights Act of 1964 forbade discrimination, but discrimination
still exists. The Voting Rights Act of 1965 outlawed poll taxes, but
somehow the voting polls are messed up. People don't know if they
are democrats, republicans, or nonpartisans. They don't know what
they are, because most of the politicians lie, and they try to cover
up their lies. The nation has changed in the last half century.

A Black president Obama being elected twice. A Black
president, but a rise in White Supremacy. Where does the nonsense
ends? You can visualize dogs of different colors getting alone, but
what about humanity getting alone? Caught on video, the late
Rodney King said "Can't we just get along." The African American
who was beaten by police officers in Los Angeles California in

1991 which led to the 1992 Los Angeles riots. Rodney King died in 2012. He was born in 1965. He was 47 years old when he died. This unnecessary violence should stop, it causes racial tension, which stirs up turbulence in our communities, our cities, and our states, and government.

In Inkster Michigan another caught on video violence of police officers beating an African-American man during a traffic stop after he ran a red light on January 28, 2015. When 57-year-old Floyd Dent was pulled over, officers yanked him out of the car with guns drawn and started to beat him. One officer even placed Dent in a choke hold. Dent was hit in the head at least 16 times while another officer tried to handcuff him. Another officer hit Dent with a taser three times. By the end of the horrific ordeal, a total of five police officers were on the scene. Come on now all of this for running a red light. Perhaps a warning or a traffic ticket was in order, but not a beating. For information and source on the website **htt://:newsone.com/31019984/ Detroit-police-beat-black-man-ran-traffic-sign/**

Malice Green was a resident of Detroit, Michigan who died after being assaulted by Detroit police officers Walter Budzyn and Larry Nevers on November 5, 1992. Both officers were later convicted for Green's death. The official cause of death was ruled to be due to a blunt force trauma to his head. Budzyn and Nevers were patrolling in Detroit in plain clothes in an unmarked vehicle. Green had pulled up to a house known for drug activity. Budzyn asked Green for his driver's license and Green had walked around the passenger side of the car and sat in the passenger seat of the car with his legs out of the doorway. Green looked through the glove compartment then grabbed something from the car's floor.

Budzyn asked Green to let go of the object. Green allegedly failed to relinquish a vial of crack cocaine. After refusing to let go. Nevers struck Green in the head with his flash light approximately 7 to 14 times during the struggle which according to local official's autopsy resulted in his death. After the struggle Green was transported to a local hospital for treatment for the head injuries sustained in the struggle where he died. A subsequent report presented by experts testifying for the defense at the trial stated that Green died of heart failure caused in part by an enlarged heart due to years of substance abuse and aggravated by the struggle with police. You can find this article on the **Video Archive** https://www.youtube.com/watch?V Also, **Wikipedia The Free Encyclopedia**.

Here again an example of brokenness. Years of your body mixed with drugs as a Black man causing your heart to be enlarged and other complications in his body was a problem. Being at the wrong place at the wrong time. Brokenness with the White police by taking the law in their own hands by overly beating a Black man. In this case both were wrong., but a Black man was killed. I have a prayer for the families of the victims who were killed by White police officers, and the family for the White police officers killed by Black men.

The Prayer: Father of all mercies and God of all consolation, you pursue us with untiring love and dispel the shadow of death with the bright dawn of life. Give courage to the families who tragically lost their love ones. Be their refuge and strength, O Lord, reassure them of your continuing love and lift them of your everlasting love and lift them from the depths of their grief into the solace of peace and the light of your presence. Your Son Jesus Christ our Savior died to destroy their death, and by his rising, life was restored to them. Your Holy Spirit, our Comforter, make darkness come to light. Come along side your people of who are living in an alien land, remind them of your eternal presence everywhere, and especially their Heavenly home and give them your comfort and strength. Amen.

Also, for all of us who may be judgmental of some type of brokenness. The Bible says in Luke 6:37 (New Revised Standard Version) "Do not judge, and you will not be judged; do not condemn, and you will not be condemned. Forgive, and you will be forgiven;" It's hard to forgive someone who brutally killed your loved one. Jesus said in his Word that we should forgive if we want to be forgiven. On the other hand, we will not be forgiven if we do not forgive. As I close out this chapter I will discuss some positive things about the theological contributions of African Americans in the next chapter. It is good to know about God which is alright, but to know God is even greater.

We get ourselves all mixed up about God even in circumstances relating to racial tension, regardless of what color we are. Hear this out, all of us, our society is brainwashed in competition. This causes selfishness. Even then there is an insecurity battle that we can't win. "The writer Christopher P. Momany said this about Paul Ricoeur."[1] Some years ago, writer Paul Ricoeur offered a provocative suggestion. "Ricoeur posited that intellectual growth might follow a three-fold pattern. First, according to Ricoeur, we accept the world as given. We inherit belief systems, ways of viewing things, and certain religious convictions. Second, perhaps, we test these inherited norms and perspectives. We may leave them entirely for a while or for good. Yet some move beyond simplistic acceptance and critical rejection to a third posture. This Ricoeur called a "second naivete." His choice of language is at once is intriguing and troubling.

Few of us want to be naïve; and many consider our earliest, simplest understandings to be just that. Many will grow beyond rigid beliefs, and many will also declare that the move beyond our first beliefs is genuine maturity. Ricoeur challenges us to consider that there is a kind of naivete that involves giving ourselves to something or someone. We cannot be isolated from each other and wrapped up in self- assured critique of the world. This third movement is dangerous. It could be used as an excuse to accept bondage once again. People often give themselves over to the same oppressive dynamics that held them long before. Yet this third movement holds promise. It can represent a brand-new giving of the self to God and others.

There is an irony here, too. Our search for the self in isolation from the outside world is doomed. Only in relationship do we find our identity. This does not mean that we discover ourselves through controlling relationships. Rather, we discover ourselves through relationships with the living God. Additionally, this is not something we invent or determine. God entered the world and gave to us before we ever considered giving our lives to God.

So, despite our understandable fear of being measured against others, there is something about us that remains unknown until illumined by an external reality. That reality is God. We are not created and set adrift. We are called into being and kept alive by holy conversation, and the voice that gives us identity comes from God. This divine address can be confused with worldly noise, but it cannot be replaced. There are plenty of competing voices out there, and they are all happy to tell us who we are. However, only God has the power to reveal our real lives.[2]

Since God has the power to reveal our lives, we cannot fight this power that reveals our lives. We are too selfish and too finite to understand God; however, we can come to know God better in his Word, and there is where he reveals himself. We can hear God's voice by understanding how the Holy Spirit moves in our being. All cultures and the works of humanity cannot and will not prosper unless we submit ourselves to God who is the author and finisher of our faith.

# CHAPTER 5

## Theological Contributions of African Americans

In the book entitled, "God Being And Liberation" by Carlyle Fielding Stewart III, he discusses some areas of concerns in Black Theology by James Cone and Howard Thurman."[1] "The question is, what is Black Theology coming from Cone, Black Theology is principally and fundamentally black and Christian: "A theology that is unreservedly identified with the goals of the oppressed community and seeking to interpret the divine character of their struggle for liberation."[2] (Stewart's Book for reading pages 1-292)

Ultimately, he states, "Christian theology is a theology of liberation. It is a rational study of the being of God in the world in light of the existential situation of an oppressed community, relating the forces of liberation to the essence of the gospel, which is Jesus Christ."[3] As a special arm of Christian Theology, Black Theology addresses the plight and struggle of black people against racism, oppression and exploitation and stresses divine liberation as the focal point of their emancipation from the "Sturm and drang" of their political and social imperilment. But it is important to note that the term "black" has connotative and denotative significance, for as Cone states, while taking seriously Paul Tillich's declarations on the symbolic nature of all theological speech, "The focus on blackness does not mean that only blacks suffer as victims in a racist society, but that blackness is an ontological symbol and visible reality which best describes what oppression means in America."[4]

Black Theology therefore is theology that addresses, through the ontological symbol of blackness, the struggles and aspirations of the oppressed, and examines prospects for divinely sanctioned liberation. It is because white racism is the principle feature of the oppression that blackness as an ontological category is linked with other similar forms of oppression. Thus, Black Theology is also, "survival theology," "passionate language" and the story of black people's "struggle for liberation in an extreme situation of oppression."[5]

Why Black Theology? Cone states: On the American scene today, as yesterday, one problem stands out, the enslavement of Black Americans. But as we examine what contemporary theologians are saying, we find that they are silent about the enslaved condition of black people. Consequently, there is no sharp confrontation of the gospel with white racism. There is, then, a desperate need for a Black Theology; a theology whose sole purpose is to apply the freeing power of the gospel to black people under oppression.[6] The appearance of Black Theology on the American scene, then, is due exclusively to the failure of white religionists to relate the gospel of Jesus to the pain and suffering of being black in a white racist society.[7]

Howard Thurman's theology illumines a special kind of liberation and that indeed he can be considered a liberation theologian, but not in the conventional sense of a James Cone or Miguez Bonino. Thurman accentuates the inner liberation of self from those forms of internal and external oppression thwarting realization and actualization of authentic existence. Unlike Cone and other liberation theologians who stress only external elements, i.e., racism, poverty, institutional oppression, etc., precluding the fulfillment of being, Thurman focuses primarily upon the internal elements of the self that both consign themselves and acquiesce to oppression. Thus, fear often operates as an internal impediment to the actualization of self as a free being. For Cone the key to personal freedom and fulfillment of being is external to the oppressed individual. So long as one is subject to and controlled by what can be termed the outer adversary, one is not truly free. Thurman states: The basis of one's inner togetherness, one's sense of inner authority must never be at the mercy of factors in one's environment, however significant they may be. Nothing from outside can destroy a man until he opens the door and lets it in.[8]

By internally conceding to the oppressive and external machinations, "one opens the door" to spiritual enslavement. The basis of human freedom is thus interior to the individual. Once the inner self is controlled and dominated by the outer adversary, one is not free. In affirming Jesus' relevance to this issue, he states: His message focused on the urgency of radical change in the inner attitude of the people. He recognized fully that out of the heart are the issues of life that no external force, however great and overwhelming, can at long last destroy a people if it does not first win the victory of the spirit against them.[9]

People can be destroyed by violence, but violence puts out, a message. "one that live by the sword will die by the sword." Unfortunately, violence is so permanently ingrained in the fabric of American society, it has become a way of life for some of us. America was birth in violence. It may perish by the very violence that points out our national birthright. The problem is that Americans never agree on the goodness of the origin for which violence is invoked. Personally, it is not good for its victims, neither does it benefit its perpetrators.

Cone responds: "When whites ask me, "Are you for violence?" my responder is: Whose violence?" "Richard Nixon's or his victims?" The Mississippi State Police or the students of Jackson State?" "The New York State Police or the inmates of Attica?"[10] Cone finds such distinctions necessary since all too often violence is identified with the oppressed and seldom with oppressors. The oppressed are victims of the violence of oppressors. The concern is whose violence shall be supported in the liberation struggle, oppressors' or oppressed. If violence is not just a question for the oppressed but primarily for oppressors, then it is obvious that the distinction between violence and non-violence is an illusory problem.[11] Violence for Cone, does not simply mean "behavior designed to inflict physical injury to people or damage to property," but is equally. . . camouflaged in such slogans as "Law and order," "freedom and democracy," and "the American way of life." This is speaking of white collar violence, the violence of Christian murderers and patriot citizens who define right in terms of whiteness and wrong as blackness . . .[12]

Elsewhere he addresses: Violence is not only what black people do to white people as victims to change the structure of living; it is also what white people did when they created a society for white people only, and what they do to maintain it.[13] The objective of liberation is to eliminate the violence of oppressors by cancelling out the dehumanizing forces of oppression. What is meant by here is there is only the question of the justified and the unjustified use of power and the question of whether the means are proportionate to the ends, and the only people who can answer the problem are the victims of injustice.[14]

Here Cone draws upon the doctrine of Just Revolution whose legitimating principles approximate the doctrine of proportionality in Just War theory. Does morality end where the gun begins? In the theory of Just Revolution, the act of violence is sought in the questions: Should the violence of Revolution exceed the violence of oppression? Of course, any evaluation of the appropriateness of violence depends upon the ones involved and their subjective determination of the relative values and effects of revolution. Liberation often overrules violence.

Yet, the oppressed resort to violence only as a final alternative. The brutality of oppression and dehumanization are so unbearable that finally, after more pacific measures of attaining freedom have failed, the oppressed embrace it as the only means of securing freedom. Simone de Beauvoir observes: by virtue of the fact that the oppressors refuse to cooperate in the affirmation of freedom, they embody, in the eyes of all men of good will, the absurdity of facticity, ethics also demands that they are suppressed. . .. Others will have to be treated like things, with violence . . .[15]

This violence of which Cone speaks is never to be fomented by hatred or vengeance. This is because the oppressed have been victims of mental and physical dehumanization, we cannot make the destruction of humanity, even among oppressors, an end in itself. Such an act contradicts the struggle of freedom, the essence of our striving. Our intention is not to make oppressors the slaves but to transform humanity. Thus, hatred and vengeance have no place in the struggle for freedom.[16]

The essence of liberation, for Cone, is that while freedom must be exacted by "any means necessary," it is not freedom where everything is permitted. Robert McAfee Brown states, "there cannot be excessive destruction for the sake of even minimally desirable ends."[17] Violence, as it therefore coincides with the doctrine of Just Revolution, can never be an end within itself, but merely a means to an end. Although the oppressed are often coerced into violent activity by their excruciating circumstances. Cone insists the principle motivation is love. The ethic of liberation arises out of love, for ourselves and for humanity.[18] Oppression has two sides. One group enlightens mankind by the thrust of itself. The other group are condemned to support it.[19]

Cone insists that reconciliation cannot occur without liberation. When black people emphasize their right to defend themselves against those who seek to destroy the black community, it never fails that so-called white Christians then ask, "What about the biblical doctrine of reconciliation?" "What about forgiveness?"[20] He goes on by saying, "We black theologians must refuse to accept a view of liberation that pretends that slavery never existed, that we were not lynched and shot, and that we were not presently being cut to the core of our physical and mental endurance." [21]

Reconciliation can only occur after liberation, for it is folly for the oppressed to reconcile themselves unto tyrants whose principle objective is their complete annihilation. "Reconciliation then is, a divine action that embraces the whole world changing our relationship with God and making us new creatures."[22] Elsewhere Cone states, "God's reconciliation is a new relationship with people created by his concrete involvement in the political affairs of the world, taking sides with the weak and helpless."[23]

Reconciliation is transformative because it catapults the oppressed in a new existence made possible through God's liberating activity. After blood has flowed in the streets, the screams have descended into silence, and the smoke of ash has vanished, the conditions for reconciliation are set, and the burden of reconstruction lies on both oppressors and the oppressed. "Yesterday we were slaves, but reconciliation means that we are free. Yesterday we were separated from God, alienated from his will and enslaved to the evils of this world. Now we are reconciled; fellowship with God is now possible because Christ through his death and resurrection has liberated us from the principalities and powers and the rulers of this present world."[24]

The content of Howard Thurman's Liberation Ethics starts out with quotes in Stewart's book on page 198. "Non-violence is not garment to be put on and off at will. Its seat is in the heart, and it must be inseparable part of our very being." **MoHandas K. GANDHI.** "And you will know the truth, and the truth will make you free." (New Revised Standard Version). "Chance has never yet satisfied the hope of a suffering people. Action, self-reliance, the vision of self and the future have been the only means by which the oppressed have seen and realized the light of their own freedom." **Marcus Garvey.**

It has stated that Thurman, like Cone, is concerned with the establishment of authentic existence for the oppressed. In contrast to Cone, however, achievement of such being occurs through the cultivation of inner strength and the development of creative potential to facilitate this movement toward wholeness, which is actualized optimally in community. Although Thurman stresses the "interior search" for wholeness, he also affirms the importance of the external search. That is, in movement toward wholeness one does not merely cultivate an inner strength for resisting evil powers and principalities but also externally confronts these powers and principalities by assuming social responsibility. But in order for individuals to effectively confront these powers, they must possess commitment and a kind of spiritual cohesiveness.

Knowing that they are children of God, they speak in truth., love and righteousness to their adversaries. Several important points must be made if we are to understand the basic thrust of Thurman's ethics. First, a universal moral order to which all persons are subjected pervades the universe. It was stated earlier that this principle is closely related to Natural Law since creatures possess an intuitive knowledge of right and wrong, and good and evil. "Thurman states:

In the first place there is the insight that life is its own restraint. The logic of this notion is that there is a moral order by which the life of the individual is bound. It is inescapable and applies to all men alike.[25] "And elsewhere he affirms: It is a terrifying truth that life is its own restraint. And that the moral law that binds in judgment the life of the individual binds the nation and race."[26]

Undergirding this moral order is the God of love and truth. Love gives all things form. God's love for us and our love for others are the motivating impetuses for movement toward community and constitute the perennial foundation of all human relationships. Truth is the cognitive counterpart of actualizing love, for our recognition and consciousness of God as truth precipitates the actualization of love in relation with others and vice versa. Love and truth are inextricably bound. One is sentient, the other cognitive. So long as love and truth are appropriated and actualized in human relations, the possibility of encroaching on the universal moral order exists, individuals tend to limit their moral boundaries.

"One of the most serious results of this deflection is in the lives of Negroes themselves. They know from cruel experience that the Christian ethic has not been sufficiently effective in the life of the Caucasian or the institutions he controls to compel him to treat the Negro as a fellow human being.[27] Through socialization and the concomitant prejudices it fosters, individuals, communities and nations develop ethical boundaries that only include members of a particular group. Thurman indicates, "One of the central problems in human relations is applying the ethic for personality in a way that it is not governed by special categories."[28] In reference to his own socialization and the resulting ethical exclusivism, he states, "Living in a frozen status established the boundaries of my ethical concern. Those who were a part of the segregated world came under the judgment of my interpretation of the meaning of religion. It made for a peculiar kind of self-righteousness. The common saying in my world was: the white man did not have any religion. By implication we did. That kept me from expecting him to act toward me as I would expect a fellow Christian to act, but curiously enough my religion did not demand of me that I act toward him as a Christian should act."[29]

Unfortunately, being a black man in American society, Thurman was himself a victim of this moral exclusion. A central problem with Christian ethics is its tolerance of racially negative attitudes which are inimical not only to actualizing community, but equally to actualizing being. Individuals and collectives are socialized and inculcated with anti-social attitudes, and so long as the "Christian" social and moral establishment does not condemn these attitudes, the disintegration of moral boundaries by racially polarized groups will never occur. Thurmond points out: Segregation is at once one of the most blatant forms of moral irresponsibility. The segregated persons are out of bounds, are outside the magnetic field of ethical concern.[30]

The assumption of Thurman's analysis is that if total harmonizing of community were to exist amongst the races, the need to establish ethical boundaries would not exist, since each racial group would view itself organically related to a larger human community and thereby morally accountable to the other. If realization of love and truth (God) in human relations (both as means of realizing community and wholeness of being) is the sum of our ethical striving then the sum is disruption of this process by choosing evil over good. Man's choice of good and evil lies in his volition (will) and freedom. For Thurman and in contrast to classical Christianity, man's sin is not due so much to an intrinsically corrupt nature as it is his manner to choose evil over good.

This problem emanates from what Reinhold Niebuhr terms "dilemma of the latitude of freedom."[31]Therefore if segregation, racism and mutually exclusive moral boundaries exist, it is because man chooses this evil over the good of actualizing community. Just as moral boundaries and their equivalents exist by choice, their disintegration may equally occur by choice.

"Important here is the process of ethical decision-making. In choosing good or evil, man can never opt for the middle path. The response must invariably be "yea or nay."[32] An apathetic response to the evil of segregation is indirectly an approbation of segregation. Ayn Rand put it this way, "The man who refuses to judge, who neither agrees nor disagrees, who declares that there are no absolutes and believes that he escapes responsibility... is responsible for all the blood now spilled in the world ... there are two sides to every issue, one ... right ... the other wrong ..., but the middle is always evil. The man who is wrong still retains some respect for truth., if only by accepting the responsibility of choice. But the man in the middle is the knave who blanks out truth in order to pretend that no choice or values exist, who is willing to sit out the course of any battle, willing to cash in on the blood of the innocent or to crawl on his belly to the guilty" ... [33]

"Good can never be compromised with evil, for "in any compromise between food and poison only death can win."[34] The response should be "yea or nay." And judgment should emanate from love and truth, for these two universal principles, exemplified principally in the relations of God and humanity, constitute the vitality and form of all human life and the universal moral order. By this love and truth are ideally the primary forces of moral judgment and the supreme rationale for

formulating the relations indispensable for community. We should all understand this formula.

In the book entitled "African American Christian Ethics" by Samuel K. Roberts in his Contents he talks about <u>foundations,</u>

sources, and contexts in his book.[35] I will attempt to share briefly these three areas. As for a framework, "Does he not see my ways, and number all my steps?" Job 31:4 (New Revised Standard Version). The present study assumes that an African American Christian ethic exists and that the exploration of the warrants and sources for normative behavior and reflection on the practical implications as such an ethic are worthwhile pursuits. The general thesis of this book is that the African American Christians have developed by virtue of their history and culture a unique ethical consciousness has emerged from the fundamental attempt on the part of African Americans to make sense of their sojourn within the context of American history. Their appropriation of Christian symbols and worldview within this experience has been foundational to the development of this unique African American Christian Ethic.

Except for the indigenous people what we call the Native Americans in North America, all persons in what we call now the United States we must realize that the religious heritage of the ancestors was formulated in other times and other places. This is the pre-Christian histories of the Europeans and Africans in ancestral homelands before destiny brought them together in a tortured relationship on the North American continent. That age begins with European expansionism in the middle fifteenth century, and at least developed events that we now call American history. These cultures coming to the new world were pagans. Yet to this day and time, many Americans, black and white, descendants of worshipers of gods, and other deities affirm the primacy of Christian faith. While white and black Christians share the same faith, the relationship between them has been anything but harmonious, to say the least.

Historically, the relationship between the European practitioners of Christian faith and captured Africans has not always been felicitous, nor has it always been free of hypocrisy. Jones continues throughout the book on pages 3- 295 to discuss the African American Christian Ethics. There is an anatomy of

American racist culture. We need to rethink the entire American way of living. In order to know where you're going, you need to know where you've been. In the first half of the nineteenth century, Protestant slave-holders would come to value indoctrinating their slaves in the Christian faith Such proselytizing proceeded out of a sense of guilt or because of attenuated sense of Christian duty or even out of a utilitarian motive like the one advanced by Charles C. Jones. A Presbyterian minister and self-styled "apostle to the slaves,"[36] Jones believed that indoctrination in the Christian faith would make slaves more docile and obedient to their holders.

While at the end of his "ministry" Jones believed that he had failed in his mission, since slaves seemed to resist his peculiar interpretation of the Bible, he nevertheless believed in the efficacy of his method and the rationale for bringing enslaved Africans into the Christian household of faith.[37] Are there "universal" tenets of truth inherent in the Christian faith that are available to all believers in the faith without regard to the particular vantage points from which they approach the faith? Or must the truths of the Christian faith always and only be perceived through the particular perspectives of those vantage points of culture? If the perception of these truths is relative to particular cultures, what does this say about the legitimacy of any presumed universals within the faith? As far as <u>Part 1 Foundations</u>, we need God as the Ground of Being. Long before we were, God was, and long after we shall have gone, God will be. We encounter God when we come into existence, but God remains after we return to dust. What does it mean to speak to God down through the ages? There is something out there that is more supreme than us. Even as we reflect the nature of God, we can see his works as the rain pours, and snow on the ground, nobody can do that but an almighty God.

The American spiritual has a song entitled, My God is a rock in a weary land, is based on the scripture Isaiah 26:4 "Trust in the Lord forever, for the Lord, the Lord is the Rock eternal." (New International Version). When you talk about the word rock it speaks to us as something strong and solid. God is our strength, and he is solid in our spirit by his presence all around us. The author "Roberts talks about the God in the Old Testament, this consciousness has the Creator walking in the garden in the book of Genesis, even displaying anger and compassion as human beings do; this God seems to have feelings, including love and hatred as humans have."[38]

The two major traditions that informed Christian theology are the Hellenistic and the Hebraic thoughts. One being classical Greek philosophy, and moving to all things as, "indefinite and without beginning," which would account for all things in the world that come to be."[39] Once having come into being, matter would be eternal. On the other hand, the Judeo-Christian tradition categorically rejected the earlier review and affirmed that time and matter would be eternal. The two forever in conflict, and therein lies a tension that continues to manifest itself in various theological problems that persist to this day as stated on page 34.

When we continue to talk about Foundations, we must realize that we have Christ as our Liberator and Reconciler. An American Negro spiritual states "O when I come to die, O when I come to die, Give me Jesus." The author Roberts mentions a few authors about the subject Jesus on page 71. "On the other hand, a Jesus for whom the future was as much a mystery, a dread and a hope as it is for us, and yet at the same time a Jesus who would say, "Not my will, but yours!"

This is a Jesus who could effectually teach us how to live, for this is a Jesus who would have gone through life's real trials. Then we would know the full truth of the saying, "No man can have greater love than this, to lay down his life for those he loves" John 15:13 (New Revised Standard Version), for we would know that he laid down his life with all the agony with which we lay it down.[40]

Nicene affirmed that there is "more" to Jesus than his human dimensions, desires, proclivities, and needs. Jesus is "very God and very man." Eventually an orthodoxy would develop that would seek to hold two seemingly irreconcilable assertions together: that Jesus was divine and human, as Soren Kierkegaard would later term it, "the absolute paradox of God-man."[41] Roberts explains on page 75 that the Logos has always been here and always will be here, much as God the Father has been here and always will be here. Hebrews 13:8 puts it less philosophically and more poetically: "Jesus Christ is the same yesterday and today and forever." Even now, to a certain extent the stuff out of which humanity comes shares in this aspect of preexistence if one appreciates the preexistence of the basic matter and building blocks of life that are constituent and basic to human life.

The talks on <u>Foundations</u> lifts up the Holy Spirit as Counselor and Inspirer. "The letter kills, but the Spirit gives life." 2 Corinthians 3:6 (New Revised Standard Version) When he (God) speaks to me now in Spirit, I move with certainty. This saying is the testimony of former slave, God Struck Me Dead. "Adolf Holl, a German Catholic scholar, has boldly declared that "without this Holy Spirit, Jesus would never become Christ, and the religion that traces itself to Jesus Christ would have had to look for another name."[42] Christians everywhere believe in the Holy Spirit.

The thrust of Chapter 4 in Robert's book from pages 99-124 is to investigate the meaning of the Holy Spirit for the ethical integrity in the life of the African American Christian believer. Mostly all Christian theological systems affirm that God, the Holy Spirit, and Christ as Son of God share a mystical unity in the Trinity. The notion of the Trinity asserts, not that there are three Gods that are worshiped, but that in one God there are three aspects.

"Geoffrey Wainwright reminds us, in the Old Testament the spirit of God or the spirit of the Lord "indicates the distinction of identity that will eventually allow the Christian church after the coming of Christ and the Pentecostal outpouring of 'Holy Spirit,' to elaborate its doctrine in a trinitarian direction."[43] The Old Testament views God as a spirit whose very essence is the spiritual. Moreover, God, as spirit, also has a spirit. God's very nature is to have one. The term "holy spirit" appears relatively few times in the

Old Testament (Psalms 51:11; Isaiah 63:10,11), it is equivalent to the more frequently used "spirit of God" or "spirit of the Lord."

The New Testament images of the spirit of God is found in the earliest of the New Testament writings, the Pauline epistles, the apostle shares two ways of understanding the Spirit. (1) Paul continues the Old Testament penchant for understanding God as one the same.[44] In Romans 9:1, Paul says, "I am speaking the truth in Christ. I am not lying; my conscience confirms it by the Holy Spirit." NRSV (New Revised Standard Version) In Romans 14:17-18, he says: "For the Kingdom of God is not food and drink but righteousness and peace and joy in the Holy Spirit. The one who thus serves Christ is acceptable to God and has human approval." NRSV (New Revised Standard Version) Thus, the New Testament continues the Old Testament tradition of identifying God as spirit and to appreciate how that spirit can inspire and prepare us for feats.

On pages 125-200 Roberts talks about **Sources.** In this 5th chapter of his book he titles this chapter as the "People of the Book." "For the word of the Lord is upright, and all his work is done in faithfulness." Psalm 33:4 NRSV (New Revised Standard Version) Go to the third of Matthew and Read the chapter through. It is a guide for Christians. And tells them what to do. This saying is "Been a Listening" which is an American Negro spiritual. Christianity, like Islam and Judaism is said to be a "religion of the book.) What is meant by this is the recognition that normative understandings of faith and practice have been written down as sacred texts.

Muslims follow the revelation of Allah and the teaching of Muhammad as recorded in the Koran; Jews acknowledge the Torah, much of it attributed to divine utterance, as foundational for an understanding of the nature of God, covenant, and community. Christians acknowledge the Holy Bible, comprising the Hebrew Bible and later writings that were prompted by the revelation of God in the life and meaning of Jesus Christ, writings that came to be known as the New Testament. As Christians, we are a "people of the book." We must realize that the Bible is a breathtaking compilation of different various sorts of literature, religious witness, and declarations of the way God has interacted with humanity and creation. Love stories; accounts of political interests, military campaigns; meditations on the nature of God, human destiny; tragedies; prophecies; poetry; and wisdom sayings. All have made their way into the book that we call the Holy Bible.

The Hebrew Scriptures are composed of twenty-four books that cover the period from the beginning of the Hebrew people to their release from Babylonian captivity, as recorded in the second volume of the book of Chronicles. On the other hand, Christians recognize the Hebrew Scriptures plus twelve other books as constituting the Old Testament. With the closing of the Jewish canon toward the end of the first century, all of the books that Christians regard as the Old Testament were gathered into one composite whole. With the closing of the New Testament canon, generally dated in the middle of the seventh, all of the sacred texts that Christians regard as constituent of a new dispensation were gathered together.

The Bible gives you instructions on how to live right. When it comes to modern Christian thought we need biblical interpretation in the early church which is hermeneutics. The first self-conscious effort devoted to hermeneutics within the early church was the so-called Alexandria school in northern Africa. The figures most closely associated with this school were Clement (ca. 150-215) and Origen (185-254), both of whom showed evidence that they were greatly influenced by Hellenistic thought and culture. In his book The Instructor (Paidogogos), perhaps "the first book which could be described as an exposition of Christian ethics,"[45]

Clement fort-rightly declares that "everything that is contrary to right reason is sin," In the Rich Man's Salvation, "Clement suggested Jesus' commandment enjoining his disciples to sell all they had to give to the poor "is not what some hastily take it to be, a command to fling away the substance that belong to him and banish from the soul its opinions about riches, its attachment to them, its excessive desire, its morbid excitement over them."[47] Origen was greatly influenced by Philo, the first-century Jewish commentator, who himself was under the sway on Hellenism. Philo and Origen introduced allegorical exegesis into their studies. There were contradictions with the biblical texts. With this going on Origen was convinced that the Bible should remain our source of faith, even if we question or try to interpret the Bible, especially problematic texts.

Such levels in any given text would require the application of a specific type of exegetical thrust in order to unlock the true meaning of that text for the reader or hearer. "The letter shows us what God and our Fathers did; The allegory shows us where our faith is hid; The moral meaning gives us rules of daily life; The anagogy shows us where we end our strife."[48] On the other hand "Catholic theological orthodoxy and hegemony with respect to the interpretation of the Bible remained relatively unchallenged until the advent of the Renaissance and the humanistic stirrings of Erasmus. A popular expression avers that "Erasmus laid the egg that Luther hatched."[49]

On the eve of the Reformation, it was clear that the interpretation of the Bible from the perspective of questioning individuals apart from the authority of any religious movement was in the offing. The work of Erasmus lifted this trend and development. After Erasmus and these early stirrings, biblical interpretation was heading in one direction: no ecclesial authority would be able to pen up the desires of individuals to interpret scripture as they were directed. For the Church to determine the meaning of the Scriptures, it actually shifted the burden for such a task from the shoulders of the church to the more modest capabilities of each individual. What was helpful was reasoning and the conservative reaction to liberalism in the thought of Luther and Calvin, who both made a distinction between the Word of God and the literal text of the Bible.

Jerry Wayne Brown commented about Luther and Calvin by saying "they developed the doctrines of inspiration and infallibility.

Instead of the Bible speaking to the Spirit-quickened heart of human beings, the Bible became the hard, infallible 'stuff' of which dogmatic systems were made."[50] Thus was born the seeds of what would come to be called Biblical literalism, or biblical fundamentalism. The era of dogmatic systems was formulated in the 18th century.

In Chapter Six of Roberts book he talks about "**The Church as the Keeper of the Tradition**" which is found on pages 151- 182 "So then, brothers and sisters, stand firm and hold fast to the traditions that you were taught by us, either by word of mouth or by our letter." 2 Timothy 2:15 NRSV (New Revised Standard Version) There's a great camp meeting on the other side. American Negro Spiritual. Without tradition it is nearly impossible for human societies to establish a sense of continuity with the past or the ability to meet effectively the challenges of the future. Even the ways and means whereby we entertain options to tackle problems in the present and those that we may confront in the future are cut off, all too often, by tradition. Even in our critical and questioning positions toward the cultures of which we are members, we must acknowledge the power and pervasiveness of tradition.

Within this problematic of the causal relationship between tradition and social institutions which includes the Church, we may already understand the two aspects of what we mean by "tradition" "As Jeffrey Stout reminds us, "the term tradition" can refer either to something handed down from generation to generation (traditum) or to the mode of transmission itself (tradito).[51] We intuit the power of traditum as in, for example of the eldest son receiving half of the inheritance. Yet tradito, that is to say, the mechanism by which the tradition is passed down, is an equally powerful component as well, although less recognized and not always understood as such, of what we mean by "tradition."

There must be social entity or mechanism by which all traditions are safeguarded and are passed down from generation to another. If, for example, a council of elders ensures the legitimacy of the inheritances, even adjudicating disputes among relatives, then that council would be tradito.

In Part III of Robert's book, he talks about **Contexts.** I will discuss Sexuality, Commitment, and Family Life which is found on pages 217-236. "Arise, my love, my fair one, and come away; for now, the winter is past, and the voice of the turtledove is heard in our land." Song of Solomon 2:10-12 NRSV (New Revised Standard Version) "There's a love feast in the heaven by and by, children There's a love feast in heaven by and by Yes, a love feast in the heaven by and by children There's a love feast in the heaven by and by. "Rise, Shine for Thy Light Is Coming" American Negro spiritual

The continuation of human life would be impossible without human sexuality. Within the African American community today, human sexuality looms large as a topic of discussion, whether it be lyrics of pop and hip-hop records, the issue of unwed pregnancy, gender wars between men and women, calls for responsible sexuality, or advocacy of rights of homosexuals. At the national level and in countless panel discussions held in hundreds of secondary schools, community social centers, sometimes even churches, the quest for a responsible sexual ethic is being explored and pondered.

Yet by the patristic era and the time of Augustine, the church exhibits a decided aversion to physical sex and human sexuality. "This aversion was the Hellenistic thought and culture of the early church. The Stoics positioned themselves the inner part of man withdrawing from the material world and its physical preoccupations in deference to ascetic, spiritual concerns. Epicureans aspired to a peace of mind forged in part by suppressing raging physical desires.[52] The early church sought converts among the Gentiles, its Jewish heritage tended to diminish while Greeks influences increased. The rising of the Gnostics, virginity was an important issue.

Paul seemed to make celibacy an ideal: "It is well for a man not to touch a woman" (1 Cor. 7:1) NRSV (New Revised Standard

Version) He also regards marriage as a concession for those who cannot live up to this ideal: "But if they are not practicing self-control, they should marry. For it is better to marry than to be aflame with passion" (1 Cor. 7:9) NRSV (New Revised Standard Version) After a sexually indulgent youth spent with a mistress, Augustine renounced his past and "exhorted humans to abrogate bodily pleasures for the higher ideal of contemplation.[53]

Another issue that confronts us as we ponder the ethical implications of our sexuality is whether the human body and our sexuality are designed primarily for procreation or pleasure. Much depends on how we resolve this issue, but unfortunately the issue is all too often framed in the context of a dichotomy. Some proponents of the pleasure thesis base their stand on the presence of organs in the human body, such as the female clitoris, the only purpose for which seems to be the sensation of pleasure.[54]

Within the Christian Community, the great commitments we make in life, the great milestones we reach in life, must at some level be grounded in the reality of the context of community. Marriage suggests that the two persons affirm mutual trust and commitment and also are in covenant within the believing community. The most important thing is to be in covenant with God because He is our Creator. The African American is lacking in the marriage relationship, because the absence of so many men from the marriage pool either through imprisonment or early death through inner-city violence further frustrates the ability of young women to find eligible partners and thus form eventual stable family lives. The ratio of eligible women to men, estimated by Harvard sociologist Orlando Paterson to be 1000 to 672, favors black men.

Roberts talks about "The Pursuit of Justice in the Courts, Markets, and Electoral Precincts" in the Context area of his book which is found on pages 257-289. But let justice roll down like waters, and righteousness like an ever-flowing stream. Amos 5:24 NRSV (New Revised Standard Version) No more auction block for me. No more auction block for me, many thousand gone. American

Negro Spiritual, we seek to discuss the challenge of securing acceptable levels of justice for African Americans within the American societal order. As we search for the discrete contexts in which the quest for justice is played out, three societal institutions come to mind. The first is what has been called the criminal justice system. Within this system are the legal, sociological, and cultural realities that inform the adjudication of cases of persons involved in this system.

To the extent to which our concern will be an assessment about the ethical considerations of the justice system and its import on the lives of African Americans is raised. A focus of concern will be an assessment of the ethical import of differential sentencing guidelines with respect to controlled substances. The second context in which the quest for American justice is played out is the area of economics. To the extent that racial prejudice inhibits the access of African Americans to the American economic system is the extent to which an ethical consideration of the economic destiny of African Americans can be assessed. A focus of concern for us that will be an assessment lead to affirmative action as a means to rectify presumed past racial injustices.

The third context for the pursuit of justice is the area of electoral politics. To the extent that racial prejudice continues to frustrate the full inclusion of African Americans in the American polity is the extent to which we must assess the integrity of the normative order that presumes to undergird American democracy. Thus, a focus of concern in this area will be an ethical analysis of the practice of cumulative voting as a mechanism to rectify inequitable voting practices in parts of the country. The burden of this area, therefore, is to assess the means whereby the American civil order can be so ordered, from a Christian ethical point of view, to ensure the full measure of juridical, economic, and political justice for African Americans and, by implication, for all Americans.

Roberts shared the following statements on page 258-259 of his book. Society can be viewed as the network of mutual expectations between individuals that ensures the self-actualization of each individual and at the same time the maintenance of the society at large. Societies work best when they can ensure that all persons will be provided the means whereby they might seek their full share of self-actualization. But societies can only do this if they themselves are maintained. A society is maintained to the extent that individuals recognize the normative value of that society and defer to its norms, values, and expectations.

It is a natural tendency for human beings for human beings to do all manner of things to maximize their self-actualization, their interests and their desires. But such tendencies, such efforts to maximize each person's liberty, if you will, must always be restrained to some extent in deference to the expectations of the society at large. On page 259 Roberts talks about that the hope of the United States becoming a civil society is an on-going hope; the "experiment" in democracy continues. The success of the experiment will depend upon whether the citizens of the American society can reasonably feel a vested interest in deferring to the common good in full knowledge that our society values and establishes the means for full rights of each citizen.

# CHAPTER 6

## Social Contributions of African Americans

In the book entitled "Negro American Heritage" it gives an excellent description of the social life of African Americans. This book is copyrighted in 1965 and 1968 by **Century Communications, Inc. San Francisco.** In its Contents it has (12) different topics from pages 5-121. These topics are worthwhile mentioning. In **Topic 1** of this book Negro tribes in ancient western Africa warred with one another. Enemy groups came over the desert and the ocean to destroy and plunder the civilizations some of the tribes developed. Because there were only trails to follow, not many were able to travel far. It was dangerous to journey on the desert and in the jungles. European slave traders captured millions of natives and sold them into slavery. Captured Negroes were shipped to America where they were forced to labor in the fields. Many tried to escape. You will find this information on pages 5-12 of **Topic 1. (Out of the Past)**

The first arrival of slaves in America was in 1619. A nameless ship, flying a Dutch flag and riding the tide in from the sea, anchored at the English settlement of Jamestown in Virginia. This was the first start of slavery. The next two hundred years a million such captives were brought to the United States of America. The African Americans were very instrumental in building this country. Negro slaves in the South were unable to fight for freedom. People in the North who worked for abolition of slavery were often discouraged. While the Civil War put an end to slavery, it did not make the Negro a first- class citizen. Negroes had little help to learn how to use their new freedom. Leaders had to work hard to gain amendments to the Constitution of the United States that would guarantee civil rights. People sought to strangle the very roots of the Negro spirit. To this end we can look ahead to strive to continue the battle of freedom and life.

With the Civil War ending in 1865, Frederick Douglas continued to dedicate his life to the problems of his race. He demanded, "As one learns to swim by swimming, the Negro must learn how to vote by voting."[1] The Emancipation Proclamation was issued by President Abraham Lincoln, January 1, 1863, declaring that all slaves in any state in rebellion were forever free. Douglas worked tirelessly for the 13th, 14th, and 15th Amendments to the Constitution, which are the backbone of civil rights even today an outstanding statesman in his old age, he continued to inspire weary and half-free Negroes in fighting for their rights. **Topic 2** talks about Freedom on pages 14-17. It's coming," the runner yelled. It's coming over the wires. The President signed."

Negro slaves in the South were unable to fight for freedom. People in the North who worked for abolition of slavery were often discouraged. While the Civil War put an end to slavery, it did not make the Negro a first- class citizen. Negroes had little help to learn how to use their new freedom. Leaders had to work hard to gain amendments to the Constitution of the United States that would guarantee civil rights. People sought to strangle the very roots of the Negro spirit. In **Topic Three** on pages 20-29 it talks about Fame and Fortune. "The real McCoy?" one asked. "What's that?" "Aw, you know swell, perfect," the other exclaimed. "My dad told me Elijah McCoy invented a deal for oiling railroad cars while they were rolling on the tracks. At the factory an invention wasn't complete unless it had the 'McCoy' mark on it. This meant it was OK. So, when we say 'It's the real McCoy', it means it's great, it's genuine.

Many Negroes, like McCoy contributed to the business of transportation in the United States. This was helpful, because transportation made it easier for ones to travel by different ways.

In the early days people of the eastern states went west until our country stretched from the Atlantic to the Pacific. Among the pioneers were Negroes- freedmen and slaves-from both the North and the South. People of all races and many nationalities helped to build the Transcontinental Railroad. One of the most distinguished Negro pioneers of California was William Leidsdorff. This Negro millionaire owned the first steamship that sailed into San Francisco Bay and up the Sacramento River. Leidsdorff Street in San Francisco was named after him. Today Negroes sail with passenger liners and on freighters that transport cargoes all over the world. Some belong to crews on atomic-powered ships.

As we look ahead Negro freedmen and slaves joined other pioneers in the difficult struggle to settle the West. Those who sailed the oceans did not have an easy life. The Pony Express riders had to have courage and endurance. Jean du Sable settled in a miserable spot on Lake Michigan which everyone else avoided. It was difficult to save enough money to start a business. Many people had to go barefooted during the early days. To reach their goals and to help their race, Negroes needed to gain an education. In 1951 the U.S. Junior Chamber of Commerce listed him as one of America's "ten outstanding young men." Johnson was reared in poverty by his mother after the death of his father. To make a long story short.

This studious lad worked hard to obtain his goal in life. Young Johnson began his first magazine, the Negro Digest in 1942. In 1945 Johnson started another publishing venture the Ebony magazine. Once he had Ebony firmly established, Johnson started Tan and Jet; then he began publishing books. The Johnson Publishing Company is accepted as one of the world's leading publishing houses. Its magazines and books depict the bright side of a Negro life. They give hope and inspiration to young people who learn that their dreams too, can come true. Over the centuries the Negro has been an important link in American business. Out of the slave ship the Negro helped to expand plantations up to the time of the Civil War. Since then Negroes have contributed their labor and their talents to help make the American way of life what it is today.

In **Topic 4** of this book it talks about "Education Is A Treasure." Pages 32-37 it explains the importance of education that is needed for the Negroes. First of all, Negroes had little opportunity to get an education. There were not enough people able to teach those who wanted to learn. Negroes could not get ahead without an education. Negro educators were forced to start with little but their own enthusiasm. Students had to help to build their own schools and to share in raising money to support them. Negroes were in need of practical education, especially agriculture. Negro universities needed better organization, better teachers, better salaries, and more books. The educators, Booker T. Washington Mary McClead Bethune, and Mordecai W. Johnson contributed highly as Negroes playing an integral part of Negro educators.

Washington started Tuskegee Institute in the 1880's. This was about twenty years since the signing of the Emancipation Proclamation. An old carpenter at the institute expressed what a good many persons thought of this man. "First Mr. Washington could put his hand on everything he wanted around town. Then he could put his hand on anything he wanted way up to New York. Before his death in 1915, Booker T. Washington, who had worked in the salt mines from the time he was nine years old and who had known nothing but poverty, became nationally and internationally known. He became the first Negro to receive an honorary degree from Harvard University, Cambridge. He walked alongside telephone inventor Alexander Graham Bell at the same time. Tuskegee Institute was one of the first independent schools to provide practical education. President William McKinley visited the school. President Theodore Roosevelt called Washington to the White House for consultation and a dinner. The King of Denmark received Washington during his European tour, and Queen Victoria of England had him in for tea and said, "Come closer, Mr. Washington, and tell me about your school. I believe you call it Tus-ke-gee."[3] Scores of people from all over the country and the world came to see and to copy what Washington had started.

About the same time, Mary McCleod Bethune was starting a school in eastern Florida. With exactly one dollar and sixty-five cents, she begged for the use of a shabby four-room cottage near Daytona Beach with five little girls and her own son. She opened her first class on October 3, 1904. She taught the students to scour and mend cracked dishes, broken chairs, and pieces of lumber. She provided beds for children left over night by picking Spanish moss from the trees. After drying and curing it, she stuffed it into corn sacks to make mattresses. Students began to grow. She needed more room. She offered two hundred dollars to a swamp ground owner who used his land as the city dump for her ownership. In addition to that she paid a five dollar down payment and five dollars a month until the balance was paid off. The owner accepted. History in the making, money came in especially $67,000.00 from James N. Gamble, son of the founder of the soap company, Proctor and Gamble; was a liberal contributor. The little primary school grew into one of the important educational institutions in the deep South. In 1922 a Methodist school for boys in Jacksonville merged with it. The two became the Bethune-Cookman College. Her original $1.65 had grown into a million-dollar investment. Before her death in 1955. She had an enrollment of six to a college of 794 students and a faculty of fifty.

In the **Topic Five** of this book is entitled "Fighting Men." Which is found on pages 39-50. During the Revolutionary War and the Civil War, Negroes were not at first permitted to enlist in the military services. Negroes often undertook the dangerous task of spying on the Confederacy. The outcome of battles often depended on the readiness of troops and the ingenuity of individual soldiers. Sometimes white soldiers resented having to salute Negro officers. It's still the same today. Thousands of heroes who served their country were unknown and not honored. There was segregation in the armed services. Negroes were not allowed to serve in the Honor Guard until 1961. In these wars Negroes could have contributed, but racism was in the way.

During the weekend, soldiers and citizens had been swarming through the narrow cobblestone streets of Boston. It was the spring of 1770. After ten years of trouble, England had sent British troops to the colonies. They were to keep the situation under control. On March 5th on a cold icy day a little after 8 o'clock a group gathered in the center of town, Crispus Attucks, a runaway slave about six feet two inches tall, headed the group. He was a sailor off of a whaling ship. He moved among the people urging them to stand their ground. Men listened when he spoke. They acted when he commanded.

Down the street came red-coated British soldiers, clearing their way with bayonets. At a signal the Americans filled the Air with their only weapons with rocks and sticks. The Red Coats opened fire. Attucks and his followers gave three cheers and moved forward. The tall Negro, an easy target was the "the first to defy and the first to die." The excitement that followed was intense. Bells of the town began ringing. Crowds of people ran out of houses into the streets shouting and crying. "The Boston Massacre," as it is called today was one of the events that led

to the American Revolutionary War. One hundred and eighteen years later, a bronze monument was erected in Boston to honor Crispus Attucks and his followers. With this all happening was the root that engaged Negroes to fight in the Revolutionary War. Negroes fought side by side with white soldiers. George Washington issued all Negroes whether slave or free not to fight in this battle. When the British offered freedom to all slaves to join the king's army. After this move Commander George Washington changed his mind. About three thousand Negroes enlisted. The government paid slaveowners a thousand dollars for each slave they permitted to fight. Then at the end of the war the Negroes were given their freedom plus fifty dollars. It is estimated that some five thousand Negro slaves and free shouldered arms. They came from every one of the thirteen colonies.

On July 17, 1862, Congress authorized President Lincoln to accept Negroes for military service. By the end of the Civil War, some 186,000 Negro slaves and freedmen had served in 449 battles. About 75 Negroes were officers. Both Negro and white ministers held religious services in tents, on board ships, in the open air, or between battles wherever they could. When men could take advantage of the opportunity, the ministers conducted schools for soldiers who could not read or write. A Scotchman slave owner named Scobell taught John the slave about everything he knew, especially reading and writing. He also bought him a banjo and taught him many Scotch songs. With his brightness and talents appeared at the U.S. Secret Service and was the first Negro operator in the Secret Service.

Many people didn't know that General George Custer had in his company a Negro named Isaiah Dorman who spent a lot of years dealing with Indians and learned their language and customs.

He served as an interpreter for General Custer, who was fighting to end attacks on white settlers by such Indian leaders as Sitting Bull, Crazy Horse, and Rain-in-the-Face. The Battle of Little Big Horn, better known as "Custer's Last Stand", lasted only twenty minutes with General Custer and his army being massacred by Sioux Indians under Crazy Horse in 1876 in Montana.

In the Spanish-American War, twenty-two years later, Teddy Roosevelt gathered a group of soldiers to fight with him. These men came all over the country and from all walks of life. They went to Cuba to fight the Spaniards and became known as the Rough Riders. In trouble with the Spaniards, Roosevelt's men needed help, because they had been lured into a Spanish trap in a canyon and were surrounded. Knowing this the Tenth Cavalry, a Negro group charged through the heavy grass without orders. They used the same tactics they had learned in Indian wars. The frightened Spaniards fled. It was Negro Sergeant George Berry of this unit who planted the American flag on San Juan Hill. Theodore Roosevelt, later the President of the United States, said of this group, "Men who can fight for their country as did these Negro troops ought to have their full share of gratitude and honor."

The United States entered World War I on April 2, 1917, under President Woodrow Wilson's Administration to fight Germany. The cause of war, Germany had sunk four American ships. Among the millions of soldiers who enlisted were almost a half million Negroes. Some 200,000 sailed for Europe. Colonel Charles Young a Negro officer served in the United States Army during World War I. Occasionally a white soldier refused to salute Colonel Young, who was his superior. In this case, Young would simply strip off his coat, place it over the back of a chair, and ask the soldier to salute the uniform. Today a tomb of Colonel Charles Young in the Arlington National Cemetery honors this man who at the time of his death, was the highest-ranking Negro in the United States Army. There were others who received special honors. Private Henry Johnson and Private Needham Roberts were the first American soldiers to win The Croix de Guerre, a French decoration, in World War I. These two men were at their posts on the dark night of March 14, 1918. Twenty Germans rated the post at which they were stationed, but the two held their ground. The New York World described this skirmish as the "The Battle of Henry Johnson." Three Negro regiments and several battalions and companies had their flags decorated for bravery. Negroes in the artillery and signal corps units won high honors.

Twenty-three years later on Sunday, December 7, 1941, the United States entered World War II, after the Japanese attack on Pearl Harbor. A Negro mess boy, Dorie Miller not being trained to fire a gun, under unusual circumstances fired down four enemy planes in which the Navy gave him credit for it. Miller was awarded the Navy Cross for having shot down the first plane. As the United States entered World War II, approximately 900,000 Negroes wore uniforms. Many Negro women joined the women's branches of the armed forces. There are thousands of unknown, Negro heroes who served the country they loved. But there were hundreds of other Negroes who performed outstanding feats and received distinguished honors. The two most outstanding Negroes in the military were and still are Brigadier General Benjamin O.

Davis, Sr., and his son Lieutenant General Benjamin O. Davis, Jr. They are the first and only Negroes to achieve rank of general in the regular army at that time. Since that cold day in March when Crispus Attucks died in the Boston Massacre, Negroes have stood and fallen with all races of men and women to defend America. They fought from sea to sea and from coast to coast to protect the Union. They fought in Europe, in Asia, and throughout the world. They fight today.

**Topic Six** talks about <u>Notable Women,</u> which is found on pages 52-59. Harriet Tubman, one of the most successful members of the Underground Railroad, was born a slave in Maryland. In her twenties she ran away to the North. But not content to enjoy freedom alone, she went back to lead her family and then her friends to freedom. On her many trips she often sensed danger and called upon God to help. He must have guided her steps all the way, for she went into Maryland and Virginia nineteen times and brought out three hundred slaves. She never lost one. Because her success inspired many to run away, plantation owners offered $40,000 for her capture. But she remained free to make another raid. This short, courageous woman started her band on its way. She took the lead, and each followed closely behind. They moved carefully, frightened at every crackling twig.

During the Civil War, she shouldered a rifle for almost three years, acting as a scout for the Union Army and recruiting troops for President Lincoln. Just as did Clara Barton, later to become the founder of the American Red Cross, Harriet Tubman went to the battlefields of the war. Both nursed hundreds of wounded men brought to the rear. They went from one suffering soldier to another, bandaging and easing pain as much as they could. They comforted the dying and took their last messages. Clara Barton asked for cloth for bandages, for ticking and making beds, for fruit and jelly, and the like. She was able to load a boxcar with supplies donated by people of the North. Harriet Tubman baked pies at night to sell so she could get money to buy food. Harriet Tubman died on March 10, 1937. A year later the citizens of Auburn, New York, paid a tribute to this remarkable woman, called "Moses of Her People." Flags flew at half- mast in her honor, and a tablet inscribed to her was placed at the front entrance of the city courthouse.

Among other Negro women who have proved their ability is Constance Baker Motley. While she was still in high school in her home town of New Haven, Connecticut, she made her decision to become an attorney. When her father asked her why, her answer was, "Abraham Lincoln said 'Law is difficult.' I want to do something difficult. The position Mrs. Motley attained by 1964 should have made her very happy. It was a difficult one. She became the Associate Counsel for the Defense Fund of the National Association for the Advancement of Colored People (NAACP). In her position she has directed legal actions to obtain civil rights for Negroes. Mrs. Motley's talents have been challenged by even more difficult tasks when President Johnson appointed her judge of a federal district court.

The preparation for such responsibility was not easy. She started her advanced education at Fisk University in 1941 because she wanted to attend a Negro college. She transferred to New York University to complete her undergraduate work. After courses at the Columbia Law School, she passed the New York bar examination, became a clerk for NAACP, did research, prepared briefs for lawyers, and planned cases. Finally, in 1962, Mrs. Motley became a full-fledged lawyer, and since then has argued and won many cases before the various courts, including the Supreme Court of the United States. Her most recent position at that time was the President of the Borough of Manhattan in New York City. At that time, she was the highest paid Negro woman in municipal government.

Another Negro woman who became successful in law was Marjorie Lawson. On October 15, 1962, she appeared in the ceremonial room of a United States District Court. With her right hand raised, she stood before an Associate Justice of the

Supreme Court of the United States as he read the impressive oath of office. She then promised to serve as the Associate Judge of the District of Columbia to the best of her ability. It was President John F. Kennedy who selected her. He knew she had worked with dependent and neglected children and had presented their cases to the Juvenile Court of the District of Columbia. He was also aware of her contribution on several government committees.

Another difficult profession, that of the medicine, has attracted Negro women. By 1964 three hundred had become some of the finest specialist in the nation. Dr. Angela Ferguson heads the research Section of Pediatrics at Howard University, College of Medicine. Dr. Jane Wright is a noted surgeon and director of cancer research at the New York University Medical Center. Dr. Hilda G. Straker is a world-famous dermatologist, and Dr. Myra Logan is a heart specialist and surgeon. Dr. Elizabeth Bishop Davis, a psychoanalyst, is in charge of the Department of Psychiatry of the Harlem Hospital in New York City, and Dr. Mary Holloway McCoo is a specialist in anesthesiology at the University Hospital in Los Angeles. Women doctors of today have the cooperation and respect that were not given early in medicine.

Through their churches, clubs, and societies, women have done so much to help improve the lives of people. One of the most outstanding women among Negroes is the beloved leader of over a hundred thousand women throughout the world. For over twenty years, Lillian Brooks Coffee has supervised the women's department of the Church of God in Christ. In 1951 she had a serious illness which left her partially blind and paralyzed. During the year that followed, she found it necessary to use an oxygen inhalator every ten minutes so that she could continue talking at meetings. Whenever she traveled, she was lifted from a train or plane and put into a wheel chair. But that fact did not keep her from journeying 100,000 miles a year.

The women's department which she has headed is the source of strength for the organization. It operates missions and schools in the United States and in the areas throughout the world.

Her women send packages of food and clothing where they are needed. In Liberia a unit of her church erected three new mission dormitories. If it had been up to most of the young people today, Madame C.J. Walker would not have been so successful in this particular business. More and more young black people of today prefer to wear their hair natural and short in Afro hair style. In 1956 the readers of Ebony elected Madam Walker to the "Ebony Hall of Fame," the first person to be so honored. She had met the requirements for such a choice. For during her lifetime, she had used her fortune to make outstanding contributions to the advancement of Negro people and the American way of life. Many women hold positions of leadership, they are not the only ones who have made important contributions. What would the world do without the mothers who rear their children and help them to become novelists, artists, and other good parents.

**Topic Seven** talks about "Men And Women In Sports." This is found on pages 62-69. Jesse Owens a Track runner of the Ohio State University was a Star of the 1936 Olympic Games. He became the first Negro American to win the triple winner in Olympiad history. During the first week in August of 1936. Owens in four straight days had made fourteen consecutive appearances. He had broken nine Olympic records and equaled one. Jesse Owens' victories were America's victories. Every time he won, the American flag was hoisted above, those fifty other competing nations. Every time he came in first, the band played the "Star Spangled Banner." For every victory, an official crowned Jesse Owens with a laurel wreath and hung a gold medal around his neck in Berlin Germany.

Owens returned from his Olympic achievements to an appreciative America. The people opened their hearts to him. His reception in New York City rivaled that of great heroes. Mayor La Guardia extended the keys of the city to him. Owens success thrilled all Americans. To them he was pride, hope, courage, inspiration all rolled into one. The entire country heaped honors upon this man from Ohio. Yet, when asked what thrilled him most about his success, he answered, "When I saw the American flag raised in victory."

About the time Jesse Owens was enjoying success as a track star, Joe Louis, a Negro boxer, suffered humiliating defeat. In what had been a shocking and stunning upset, considered the biggest in boxing history, Max Schmeling of Germany had knocked him out. For the next two years Joe Louis suffered ridicule, torment, and embarrassment. During that time, he fought his way back to the top. And now Joe Louis had a second chance. New York City was bulging with boxing fans and sport celebrities. Almost every square foot of 49th Street near 8th Avenue was crammed with people who had come to see the return match. Managers, trainers, judges, sports writers all in the boxing world who could possibly get to the fight scene had come. Milling along the sidewalks and gathering in the cafes, the people exchanged opinions and made predictions. "Max Schmeling is inspired by the feeling he's leading a new race movement, but watch out," someone said. "He believes he's a special representative. He'll be hard to beat." Another replied, "If anybody's morale is important, it's Joe's. You know Schmeling's been laughing at him and saying he's afraid. Joe's mad. He doesn't talk much but watch out. He's waited two years for this, and waiting hasn't been easy." As the story tells Louis attacked Schmeling quickly in the 1st round and within two minutes and four seconds, the referee raised Louis' hand in victory. Louis held the heavyweight championship for eleven years, longer than any other fighter at that time.

In 1945 Branch Rickey, the man who gave Jackie Robinson a chance in baseball broke an "unwritten law" when he signed a Negro, Jackie Robinson, to a playing contract. It was the most controversial sports development of the century. All Negro Americans seized upon Jackie Robinson as their idol and symbol of racial progress. This break-through seemed, at least, to be an approach to the realization of the dreams of full-fledged citizenship. It seemed the fulfillment of promises made in the Emancipation Proclamation. If Jackie Robinson made good, it meant escape from segregated baseball. The rest is history. Jackie

Robinson became one of the all-time greats in major league baseball. He was known as the man who broke the color line, the man who, by enduring the burdens heaped upon him because of his race, had opened the doors to the "Golden Era in Sports."

Three years later, in the spring of 1948 the family of Willie Mays knew that he would graduate from school. They had a family conference. They wanted to know what Willie wanted to do. Everybody was talking about the performance of Jackie Robinson. Out of this conversation Willie Mays said he wanted to play baseball. Years later he did. Sports writers have stated that Mays plays baseball "with a boy's glee, a pro's sureness, and a champion's flare." Willie Mays has become legendary. What part is Willie Mays is hard to say. Without throwing a ball, Mays halts base runners with his reputation. Just by standing out in center field, he raises his team's spirits and depresses his opponents'.

In 1955, as a member of a good-will tennis team sponsored by the state department, Althea Gibson went on a southeast Asia tour. She became the principle attraction of the group. In 1957 she won the coveted British Wimbledon singles championship. For this, England's Queen Elizabeth shook Althea's hand and said, "My congratulations." Furthermore, the queen expressed her concern for the tennis player by adding, "It must have been terribly hot out there." Althea Gibson's name was engraved on a gold salver, along with the names of previous Wimbledon champions. This feat was repeated in 1958. Thousands of people will always remember Miss Gibson not only for her great ability to play tennis, but also for her serene gracious manners even in defeat.

A few years later another tennis player made headlines. A magazine, World tennis, in its November 1963 issue, carried a coverage page picture of him entitled, "Arthur Ashe, Promising Youngster." Arthur Ashe, Jr. from Richmond, Virginia, began playing tennis with an old abandoned racquet he found in an empty lot. He had no formal tennis instruction until he entered the University of California at Los Angeles. But soon his college coach described him as being "on the threshold of world-championship tennis." Whether Arthur Ashe reaches this pinnacle of success or not, he has already contributed much by participating in an area that attracts attention and meeting competitive stresses with quiet dignity. In 1964 Ash became the first Negro to be named on the American Davis Cup Squad. In August of the same year he was nominated for the Martini and Rossi International Sportsmanship Award for his conduct on and off the tennis courts. In January 1965 the United States Lawn Tennis Association Men's Ranking Committee placed him in the Number 3 position. Little is said about Jim Brown, but during the time of Arthur Ashe Jim Brown had gained more running yardage on the football field than any other player in professional football while playing with the Cleveland Browns. Also, Bill Russel, graduate of the University of San Francisco, nationally-known basketball player, and winner of many awards was an excellent basketball player with the Boston Celtics.

**Topic Eight** talks about Science, The World Of Wonder on pages 71-82. Since the time of slavery some Negroes were learning about medicine through study and practice. One of these was James Derham. He was born in Philadelphia in 1762. He was sold several times to different doctors. Since he could read and write he was able to mix medicines and to perform simple services for patients. His last owner, Dr. Robert Dove of New Orleans, helped Derham in his medical career and even freed him on easy terms. Derham came to know a great deal about medicine. Finally, he opened up his own practice in New Orleans. Since those days Negroes have contributed much in the field of medicine. Medical schools for Negroes were started after the Civil War, graduating many doctors. Dr. A. T. Augusta was the first Negro surgeon in the United States Army. Dr. Daniel Hale Williams trained to be a barber, but later he studied medicine. He was the first surgeon in America to operate successfully on the human heart. Dr. Louis T. Wright, a police surgeon of New York City, achieved fame for his work on head injuries. Dr. Theodore K. Lawless studied in Europe and is now the director of his own clinic for skin diseases. His patients were people of all kinds. They were poor, middle class, and wealthy. Dr. Samuel L. Kountz performed kidney transplants. He was appointed chief resident in surgery at San Mateo General Hospital, in San Mateo, California. In 1965 he became a full-time faculty member at Stanford University School of Medicine. Dr. Charles Drew was interested in the study of blood. He experimented and discovered that blood could be stored indefinitely through refrigeration. It would remain fresh and could be used for transfusion later. Because of his research, volunteers can today donate their blood to be stored in "blood banks" and used whenever and wherever necessary.

The city Washington D.C. is wheel-shaped by Benjamin Banneker, a Negro mathematician, and Major Pierre Charles L'Enfant a French engineer, together with others, could hardly have foreseen in 1791, Washington D.C. Banneker induced the plans, including the minor details by memory, for he had helped to survey the land and to plot the plans. As an astronomer Banneker he published an annual almanac predicting the weather, eclipses of the sun and moon, and other information, which would attract much attention in the United States as well as in Europe. Benjamin Banneker would go down in history as a great American mathematician and scientist.

Dr. George Washington Carver learned a great deal that could help farmers. He suggested that if they would rotate crops, the land would rebuild itself. Instead of raising cotton every year, he suggested they raise peanuts some years. In a few years Dr. Carver found hundreds of things that could be made from peanuts, such as milk, flour, candy, soap, oils, dye, ink, paper, and other products. The next time you have a peanut butter sandwich think of Dr. Carver. In addition to the peanut, he also found that you could produce a lot of things out of the sweet potato. Out of the sweet potato he produced rubber, flour, starch, and even vinegar and shoe blacking and more. Right down to the present day, Negroes have done outstanding work in science. Dr. Percy Julian is one of the country's leading scientists. His numerous scientific discoveries have been a service to mankind. One of his most dramatic contributions has been his research in the field of "wonder drugs" to combat rheumatic fever and arthritis. Other discoveries are effective in the fight against a number of diseases. In 1928, Joseph Blair at the age of twenty-four sent plans for rockets to the United States government. They thought his plans were fantastic and also impossible. The Navy took three of his inventions and marked them "top secret." Today, Negroes are working in all fields of science. They work as marine biologists, space engineers, physicists, biologists, designers, and bridgebuilders. There are far too many outstanding scientists to name them all.

**Topic Nine** The World's A Stage on pages 83-98 A famous man name Bill Robinson was a great dancer. His love of live, and his dancing ability made him one of the most popular entertainers in America. Much time has passed before he became known as "Bojangles." In 1924 he was making $4,000 a week in vaudeville plus $3,500 for cabaret engagements. He was in movies with Shirley Temple and taught her how to dance. To top that off he made over fourteen moving pictures for Hollywood. These movies were shown in cities all over the United States and in Europe. Other Negroes made names for themselves by dancing by dancing. But it was Bill Robinson who became the best known. During his seventy-one years, he earned several million dollars, most of which he gave to charity.

Louis (Satchmo) Armstrong noted for his horn was sent on a tour in 1960 for a nine-week's good-will tour. They lifted him to a kind of throne. His performances so aroused the thousands of listeners that the police begged him to play slower music. He went into other areas of Africa to equally enthusiastic welcomes. Louis (Satchmo) Armstrong, the King of Jazz who had conquered the world with his kind of music, returned to the United States to jobs that paid him $500,000 a year, but he also continued to make trips abroad. His style of playing, his warmth and humor, and his simplicity have been etched on records where they can always influence players of the golden trumpet.

Negroes have contributed a great deal in the field of major musical composition. William Grant Still wrote more than twenty works for large symphony orchestras and a number of operas. Duke Ellington, pianist, has composed for the Broadway stage as well as concerts. He has made personal appearances, played for radio and television, and has made recordings. There is W. Count Basie, composer, band leader, pianist, who in 1939 won the most Popular-Band-Musician Award. Ulysses Kay, composer and conductor, wrote concertos and symphonies that won him honors. Dean Dixon gained recognition as a conductor in America and abroad.

Jazz, the blues, and the spirituals are the special contributions of Negroes to the field of music. These forms of music, however, have attracted musicians of many backgrounds. One of the most successful is jazz. Many individual Negroes have become well known. Many Negroes whether they had training or not have created music. They sang because singing was as natural a means of expression as speaking. They sang at work, putting words to rhythmical tunes that helped them to forget monotony of their tasks. They sang about their sorrows, expressing grief for loss of money or for misbehaving or for disappointment in love. Such songs were sung all over the South. If they were good others would repeat them. Many were sung a few times and then they were forgotten. All of them would have been lost and someone who had interest saved them. In the 1900's W.C. Handy collected rhythm tunes of the southern docks and levees. He gathered them at tobacco factories and the corn fields. He got them from wherever Negroes worked and spent their time. As he put the songs down on paper, he wanted to represent the typical Negro voice slur. To do so, he introduced a flat note into the regular scale and called it a "blue note." The treatment gave melodies a mournful tone, and the term blues became the accepted name for a new type of popular music. The people of Memphis honored this musician after his death in 1958 by erecting a statue in one of its parks. It stands as a tribute to the "father of the blues." Many singers, regardless of race, include a spiritual or two in their concert programs, and audiences wish there were more. Just to name a few were Marian Anderson, the Fisk Jubilee Singers, Mahalia Jackson, Leontyne Price, and Nat King Cole.

In the acting world was Ethel Waters, also a singer. Believing that God helps those who help themselves, she always did her part, and he never failed her. Sidney Poitier, Harry Belafonte, Leslie Uggams, were very good actors, especially Sidney Poitier who received an Oscar as the best male leading actor of the year for his part in Lilies of the Field. This was awarded to him on April 13, 1964. His role was Homer Smith in "Lilies of the Field." As he accepted the golden statuette, Poitier said, "It's been a long journey to this moment. I want to thank a lot of people for making it possible." Chance had made Sidney Poitier an American rather than a British citizen.

**Topic Ten** Of The People, By The People, For The People is found on pages 99-108. Some white people thought Negro officials would be the downfall of the United States Congress. "It will be the downfall of the white race if Revels is admitted," one senator argued. He is not qualified for the position. A Negro is not a citizen." "Nonsense," another senator said. "Negroes are citizens by a higher law? Moreover, they fought for and helped to save the Union." Then came the moment everyone had been waiting for. The president of the Senate called for the vote. When the count was completed, the decision was 48-8 to admit Revels. A messenger was sent to notify Revels. As the new senator entered the Chamber, people sitting in the gallery rose. It was 4:40 in the afternoon as he walked down the long aisle to be sworn in as the as the first Negro senator. This all happened on February 15, 1870 in the Senate Chambers at the Nation's Capital.

All over the country, Negroes stepped out of slavery to become leaders of their race, but only for about ten years. An ex-slave, Blanche Kelso Bruce held a seat in the United States Senate. P.B.S. Pinchback, son of a Mississippi planter, served as lieutenant governor and then as acting governor of Louisiana. He held more offices at that time than any other Negro after the Civil War.

As years went by Negroes filled very few government positions. Nor did they have equal rights. Segregation was again imposed in restaurants, in hotels, in buses, in schools, and in many other places. It was during this period that William E. B. DuBois was born and grew to manhood. He accomplished degrees from Fisk and Harvard Universities. After two years in Germany, he returned to Harvard, which in 1895 granted him at the age of twenty-seven the first Ph.D. awarded a Negro.

Dubois taught history for many years at the Atlanta University in Georgia and wrote extensively His essays in the Atlantic Monthly, later collected and published as the Souls of Black Folk, more than any other publication influenced his people. He believed Negroes needed to train for leadership. He was the leader of the National Association for the Advancement of Colored People, simple because in North Carolina they didn't permit Negroes to vote. This disturb him. Another Negro who labored a long time was Thurgood Marshall, a lawyer licensed to present cases in the highest court of the land. He traveled about 50,000 miles yearly fighting racial discrimination, especially segregation in public schools. Because of his hard work and determination. The decision was unanimous. The justices of the Supreme Court of the United States had reversed the "separate but equal" decision of 1896. In their opinion separate schools could not be equal. This decision was made on May 17, 1954. Thurgood Marshall is now the Solicitor General of the United States, the first Negro to be appointed to this post.

Other Negroes such as E.W. Brooke of Boston Massachusetts was elected Attorney General, the second most powerful office in the state. He entered the race with the odds against his chances winning. Brooke was a Republican in a Democratic state. He was a Protestant in a Catholic state. He was a Negro in a state with ninety-eight percent white population. But he won! In 1966 E.W. Brooke won another election in Massachusetts and became the first Negro senator since Reconstruction. The Reconstruction Period for historical purposes was when northern armies were placed in each of the southern districts. Negroes were given the right to vote and most southern whites could not since they had supported the Confederacy. There had never been a period like this between 1867-1877, which the North brought an end by removing all its armies. Out of the ashes of this period arose a new South, somewhat like the old.

In Connecticut, General Lamb was elected a state treasurer. His campaign was a proof, too, that white people will vote for Negro candidates. He said, "This is in part a recognition that the Negro citizens of our country have earned the right to be considered a part of the American community. Even more, it is in recognition of the idea that all of our citizens are entitled to have earned the right to be considered a part of the American community. One of the most outstanding young men was Carl T. Rowan climbed high in government positions. He won numerous awards both at home and abroad for his newspaper reporting. He wrote books and became a popular lecturer. In 1961, he gave up his forty-thousand-dollar-a year salary for a State Department job which paid him $18,450. He became a celebrity. His official traveling was remarkable with his impressive speeches. His philosophy was that he believes the young American ought to work hard at developing his ability to read and to speak. One must want to move into this rapidly expanding field. On January 21, 1964, President L. B. Johnson appointed Carl T. Rowan to the position as the Director of the United States Information Agency. This made Rowan the most influential Negro in the United States government.

**Topic Eleven** <u>Creative Minds And Hands</u> is found on pages 109-120. Langston Hughes was a poet and author of many books. Phillis Wheatley made history in 1834 by being the first Negro to have collection of Poems to be published in the United States. In 1896, Paul Laurence Dunbar published a collection entitled Lyrics of Lowly Life and became the first nationally known Negro poet. By this time, James Weldon Johnson had been writing poetry. One of the best-known Negro artists is Jacob Lawrence. By 1938, he completed a series of thirty pictures showing the life

of Frederick Douglas, the Negro orator, and another thirty about
Harriet Tubman. Through all of his paintings he showed the good
and the bad things of life. He also taught painting to students at
Brandeis University in Waltham, Massachusetts. There is also
other Negro artist too numerous to mention. However, Negro art
depicts not only Negro aspirations, but facets of Negro life, and
Negro involvement with the community. Much of the Negro art is
an interpretation of social conditions and of the world as the artist
sees it.

**Topic Twelve** Men To Match Mountains is found on pages
121-127. Dr. Ralph J. Bunche was a representative of the United
Nations to restore peace between the Jews and the Arabs in 1948.
He did hard work at this task. Honors came to him from all parts
of the country. In 1950 he received the world's highest honor, the
Nobel Peace Prize. Mr. Bunche went to Harvard and became the
first Negro to receive a PH. D. in political Science. To get all of this
wasn't easy. It was a struggle of many years shining shoes, selling
newspapers, working as a houseboy, and a janitor. He reached
his goal by reading piles of books that gave him knowledge. In
his years of struggle, he had developed strength of character,
perseverance, and a lively humor, which was his grandmother's gift
to him. Because of refusing to give up her seat for a white passenger
on the bus, Rosa Parks in 1955 was arrested. The news spread and
within hours the Negroes embarked upon a bus boycott in the city
of Montgomery Alabama.

During that time the boycott committee became the
Montgomery Improvement Association and the Reverend Martin
Luther King, Jr., became its president. With this going on King's
home was bombed. The Negroes were violent about this ordeal, but
with King's non-violent appeal he calmed the riotous people down.
In less than a year the Supreme Court upheld a ruling that forbade
segregated seating in Alabama buses. Dr. King had a dream, and
his dream speech was before 200,000 people who gathered at the
Lincoln Memorial in which the author did not state the date of this

happening. This is very significant to mention this date which is August 28, 1963. This was a call for an end of racism and a call for the civil rights and economic rights in the United States. Right now, it is still a problem here in 2018. The Dream Speech goes something like this. "I have a dream," Dr. King said then, "that one day in the red hills of Georgia the sons of former slaves and the sons of slave owners will be able to sit down at the table of brotherhood. I have a dream," he added, "that my four little children will one day live in a nation where they will not be judged by the color of their skins but by the content of their characters." To help to make this dream come true, Dr. King practiced the policy of non-violence to fight the battle to end racial segregation in the United States. He was a long-time disciple of the late Mahatma Gandhi, whose similar philosophy helped India to win her freedom.

On January 3, 1964, Time, a weekly news magazine, named Dr. King the 1964 Man-of-the Year. On October 14, 1964, the Oslo Nobel Institute of Norway awarded him the Nobel Peace Prize for his leadership of the United States civil- rights movement. Dr. King, winning it at 35, was one of the youngest to receive such recognition. King donated the $53,000 prize money to the civil-rights movement. Dr. King was assassinated by a bullet on April 4, 1968 in Memphis Tennessee at the Lorraine Hotel. On the balcony of the Lorraine Hotel, in Memphis, Tennessee, where Dr. King was slain, there is a marble plaque reading: "They said one to another, behold here cometh the dreamer. Let us slay him and we shall see what becomes of his dreams." When Americans learn to understand and respect one another, the dreams this man of non-violence pursued in his life will at last be realized.

From the gains that have been in human rights have been achieved by the diligent and sacrificial work of all those who believe in the basic principles of human dignity and God-given rights. We have come a long way. We still have a long way to go, for every one of us must learn to recognize each individual as a human being regardless of his race, creed, or national origin. Then, and only then, will we begin to realize our true American dream. All of us need to take a stand when it comes to being an American. We do not fall down, stand! We are a strong nation.

## Triumph Over Adversity Rise Above the
## Story of The Tuskegee Airmen

We need to aim high and reach for the sky. And the above title, you can get this information by visiting www.redtail.org or calling 1-888-928-0188. The Tuskegee Airmen were the first African American aviators in the U.S. Army Air Corps. Included in the Tuskegee Airmen are pilots, bombardiers, navigators, flight trainers, and support personnel working together to keep combat airplanes in the air. For historical purposes, in 1941, a few men of color were training on airfields in Tuskegee, Alabama, to fly combat missions for the U.S. Army. At this critical time, African Americans had never served as aviators for the military. Segregation, or "Jim Crow," laws segregated the military, schools, and public places. "White Only" signs created barriers for African Americans, but the Tuskegee Airmen were determined to **RISE ABOVE** racial barriers and serve their country, a country they loved and believed could change for the better. The Tuskegee Airmen were not only fighting against the Nazis in Europe but against racial discrimination here at home.

Unfortunately, many people do not know about the Tuskegee Airmen. I will share this story about these heroes who taught America to **RISE ABOVE** barriers. When World War II erupted in Europe African Americans were not permitted to fly, because reports were saying that the black race was not capable of flying or serving in other combat positions. These claims were false. Because of the civil rights activists, the U.S. Army Air Corps started an experimental school at the Tuskegee Institute in Alabama. In 1940 there were 13 cadets. The challenging tests only five men passed tests and check rides to become the first Tuskegee Airmen. Other cadets joined. Successful graduates were assigned to one of four groups, forming the 332nd Fighter Group. Under the leadership of Colonel Benjamin O. Davis Jr., men trained around the clock to master skills in aerial combat. In 1943, following the 99th, the 332nd was sent to Italy to escort bombers, protecting them from Nazi combat airplanes. This group called the Red Tails did so well that they were requested above white escort pilots. By 1946, 996 aviators were successfully trained at Tuskegee Airfield. Together they learned to fly and maintain military aircraft for the U.S. Army Air Corps. The Tuskegee Airmen flew 1,578 missions during World War II. Awarded with high military honors, their achievements include the Distinguished Flying Cross, Silver Star, Purple Heart, and Congressional Gold Medal, the highest recognition for national contributions.

**Breaking Down Barriers**- The Tuskegee Airmen continued to break down barriers for African Americans after World War II. Their accomplishments paved the way for greater changes in America. In 1948, President Harry Truman issued an order to end segregation in the United States military. This legislation led to greater social justice in the civil rights movement, including desegregation of schools, abolishing "Jim Crow" laws, and enforcing voting rights. All of the Tuskegee Airmen worked together to prove that African Americans deserved the opportunity to succeed, and by doing so many of them went on to earn degrees as doctors, entrepreneurs, and educators. Those who stayed in their military careers earned high rank, including two four-star generals.

The Tuskegee Airmen fought racism just as effectively as they fought the Nazis of World War II. Benjamin O. Davis Jr. once said, "The privileges of being an American belong to those brave enough to fight for them." With persistence, patience, and skill, the Tuskegee Airmen won a major victory against racism creating a greater sense of unity in the United States of America. Racism endangers people's freedom: the freedom to be judged for their ability instead of their color, to be offered fair opportunities, and even to believe in themselves. It creates an invisible wall between people, threatening fellowship. The Tuskegee Airmen have six guiding principles they are: **Aim High, Believe in Yourself, Use Your Brain, Be Ready to Go, Never Quit, and, Expect to Win**.

**Aim High**- Aiming high means setting goals that lead to extraordinary achievement and, in many cases, being the first to achieve those goals. Benjamin O. Davis Sr. was the first African American general in the United States Army. He taught his son Benjamin Davis Jr. to aim high toward ambitious goals. His son did just that. No African American had graduated from West Point in the 1900s, and other students resented him. The students were trying to make him quit They underestimated Benjamin Davis. Four years later Davis became the first African American to graduate from West Point in the 20th century. With his great determination he attended Air War College and was the first African American to graduate from the Air War College. He worked his way up to be promoted as a four-star general. He continued to aim high.

**Believe in Yourself**- General Daniel "Chappie" James always knew that he was a winner. He expected nothing less from himself. He once wrote, "I am a citizen of the United States of America. I am not a second- class citizen a no man here unless he thinks like one, reasons like one or performs like one." Chappie knew that if he was going to soar over obstacles, he had to believe in himself. Many people believed that African Americans did not have the ability needed to become aviators. Despite their doubts, Chappie had confidence that he would succeed as a In Freeman Field in Indiana, Chappie learned that the African American officers were not allowed to enter the officers club reserved for white men only. Chappie and a group of African American officers challenged segregation by entering the officers club, they were arrested and charged with mutiny and disobedience. Thurgood Marshall an African American worked on this case and won. This was a major victory in the battle for civil rights in the military. Chappie climbed in rank as a pilot He was promoted to the rank of four-star general, the first African American four- star general in the history of the United States Air Force.

**Use Your Brain**- Lieutenant Colonel Lee "Buddy" Andrew Archer used his brains when odds was against him. Like many others the Army Air Corps rejected African Americans to become pilots. However, when the opportunity came alone for an all-black flight unit at Tuskegee Army Airfield, he applied for cadet training and was accepted. He earned his wings as a pilot. He learned from Wendell Pruitt one of the best flyers of the 302$^{nd}$ Squadron. The two of them completed many successful attacks on enemy planes, becoming known as "The Gruesome Twosome." In 1944 he used that skill to shoot down three German fighter aircraft, becoming one of only four World War II pilots to accomplish that feat. He received several awards including the Distinguished flying Cross and the Legion of Merit.

**Ready to Go**- Using money saved and borrowed, "Chief" Alfred Anderson bought his own airplane. Before long, Anderson taught himself to take off and land. Anderson had taught himself to fly, so when the military was ready to recruit African American pilots, he was ready to go. Recruited by the Army in 1940, Anderson was the first Chief Civilian Flight Instructor. He was good at what he did. In 1941, First Lady Eleanor Roosevelt was touring the Tuskegee flight Chief Anderson showed Eleanor Roosevelt that African American pilots were just as good as white pilots. After the flight with Chief Anderson Mrs. Roosevelt was convinced that African American pilots could fly. Taking a picture with the Chief, people who saw this photo gained confidence in the ability of African American combat pilots.

**Never Quit**- Lieutenant Charles H. Debow was one of the original Tuskegee Airmen to earn his wings. No matter how difficult the flight training might be, Debow would never quit until he soared above the very fields of Alabama where his ancestors worked as slaves. Many times, the Army turned him down for enlistment even with a pilot's license. Debow received an opportunity for the first all- black flight training program. He worked consistently to earn his silver wings as a pilot. He knew that he could never quit, paid off.

**Expect to Win**- Colonel Charles "Mack" Edward McGee expected to win. It is no surprise that his motto, "Do while you can," inspired him to be an unstoppable fighter pilot, not just in one war, but in three. He began his career in 1942. He served in World War II, The Korean War,

and the Viet Nam War. Expecting to win, Charles McGee flew 409 missions for the U.S. Army Air Forces and is the only one who flew 100+ combat hours in each of the three wars. You can succeed if you **Aim High, Believe in Yourself, Use Your Brain, Be Ready to Go, Never Quit, and Expect to Win.**

**Reveille for the Soul Prayers for Military Life by Marge Fenelon Liguori Publications 2010** This small booklet of prayers is written by those who served and are still serving in our armed forces. Reveille for the Soul provides support and solace for those serving in their country, as well as those who served before them. I, Chaplain Lieutenant Colonel Ted Whitely of the Air

National Guard have a published prayer on pages 28-29. The title of this prayer is, "Physical And Mental Fatigue." God, We have so many demands put upon us every day, particularly as families dealing with the challenges of deployment and separations. Help me God, to understand that while circumstances can drain our resources and leave us depleted, you are always there for us. You've promised that life will not leave us as empty vessels or dry up our spirits. As we face these demands each day, remind us of our inner resources and strength. Greater are you within us that anyone who is outside of us.

We can become physically and mentally drained, but we pray to you, O God, to supply us with divine strength. Our economy can become warped, but our richness and glory will move us beyond that. Something positive came come from negative situations. We can come from mental fatigue to mental strength. Page 28. We can come from emotional strain to emotional strength. God, help us to place positive thoughts into the midst of negative messages that cripple our spirit. God, since you are the great supplier, we will come to you for our needs. We thank you, God for placing people on this earth who can and will pray for us. You told us in the Scriptures that if we pray for one another, you will heal us. (See James 5:16.) God, there is a saying that helps me during the day: "Little prayer, little power; no prayer, no power; but a lot of prayer, a lot of power." This power comes from you, God, and I need it every day to get by for myself and for those around me. Amen. Page 29. As an African American I have served over 25 years in four wars, Viet Nam, Desert Storm, Enduring Freedom, and the Iraq War mainly as a Chaplain. But most importantly I have served over 41 years as a Pulpit Pastor in the vineyard of the Lord. I am retired from both ministries but still serving the Lord. And by the way I am a Tuskegee Airmen Chaplain. I give thanks to the Lord for this dissertation and all of its components.

## Glory! Glory! Glory To His Name! Song
## Writer: Dr. Theodore D. Whitely, Sr.

Glory, glory, glory to his name
Glory, glory, glory to his name

Sing a song of praises in his name
Sing a song of praises in his name

Glory, glory, glory to his name
Glory, glory, glory to his name
Worship, worship, worship in his name
Worship, worship, worship in his name

Glory, glory, glory to his name
Glory, glory, glory to his name

Praying, praying, praying in his name
Praying, praying, praying in his name

Glory, glory, glory to his name
Glory, glory, glory to his name

Preaching, preaching, preaching in his name
Preaching, preaching, preaching in his name

Glory, glory, glory to his name
Glory, glory, glory to his name

Teaching, teaching, teaching in his name
Teaching, teaching, teaching in his name

Glory, glory, glory to his name
Glory, glory, glory to his name

There is power, power, power in his name
There is power, power, power in his name

Glory, glory, glory to his name
Glory, glory, glory to his name

Jesus, Jesus, Jesus is his name
Jesus, Jesus, Jesus is his name

Glory, glory, glory to his name
Glory, glory, glory to his name

Glory, glory, glory to his name
Glory, glory, glory to his name

## Chapter 1 Notes "The Black Church Spirituals and Gospels"

1   J Alfred Smith, Essays The Ecumenical Nature of African American
    Church Music African American Heritage Hymnal (Chicago:GIA
    Publications, 2001)
2   J. Jefferson Cleveland and William McClain, Songs of Zion Hymnal
    (Nashville: Abingdon Press, 1981), p.73.
3   Ibid
4   Wyatt Tee Walker, Somebody's Calling My Name (Valley Forge, PA.:
    Judson Press, 1979), pp. 127-131.
5   Tony Heilbut, The Gospel Sound, New York: Simon and Schuster, 1971).

## Chapter 2 Notes "African American Worship"

1   Albert J. Raboteau, Slave Religion. The "Invisible Institution" in the
    Antebellum South (New York: Oxford University Press, 1978)111.
2   Ellen G. White, The Great Controversy (Nampe, Idaho: Pacific Press Pub.
    Assn; 1911) 577, 578.
3   E. Franklin Frazier, The Negro Church in America (New York: Schochen
    Books, 1964), 6.
4   Melville J. Herskovits, The Myths of the Negro Past (Boston Beacon Press,
    1941), 207-260.
5   Raboteau, 58, 59, 86 See also Eugene Genovese, Roll, Jordan, Roll. The
    World, The Slaves Built (New York Pantheon Books, 1974).
6   Pedrito Maynard-Reid, Diverse Worship-African-American Carribean and
    Hispanic Perspective": (Downers Grove, III Intervarsity Press, 2000), 61, 63.
7   James Cone, for my People. Black Theology and the Black Church (Mart-
    Knoll, NY Orbis Books, 1984), 24.
8   Martin Luther King, Jr, Strength to Love (New York-Harper and Row,
    1963), 48.
9   Cleophus LaRue, The Heart of Black Preaching (Louisville. Westminster
    John Knox Press, 2000), 3, 5.
10  James Cone, Speaking the Truth. Ecumenism, Liberation and Black
    Theology (Grand Rapids William B. Lerdmans Pub Co, 1986), 140.
11  J Wendell Mapson, Jr, The Ministry of Music in the Black Church (Valley
    Forge, PA Judson Press, 1984), 40.

12　Melva Wilson Costen, African-American Christian Worship (Nashville Abingdon Press, 1993), 18.

13　Maynard-Reid, 61.

14　Costen, 126.

15　William D. Watley. Singing the Lord's Song in a Strange Land (Grand Rapids, William B. Erdmans, 1993), 22, 23.

16　James Cone, God of the Oppressed (San Francisco Harper and Row, 1975), 144.

17　Frazier, 29-46.

18　Costen, 126.

19　Watley, 20.

20　Harold A. Carter, The Prayer Tradition of Black People (Valley Forge Judson Press, 1976), 53.

21　Eric Lincoln and Lawrence H. Mumiya, The Black Church in the African-American Experience (Durham Duke University Press, 1990), 346.

22　Mapson, 20.

23　Costen, 45.

24　James Cone, God of the Oppressed (San Francisco Harper and Row, 1975), 58.

25　Cleophus LaRue, The Heart of Black Preaching (Louisville. Westminster John Knox Press, 2000) 1, 6-12.

26　Calvin B. Rock, Black SDA Preaching Balanced Betwixt and Between? Mtnt/ try, September 2000, 5-10 For another important Perspective of Black Preaching, see Leslien Pollard, "African-American Preaching Saga and Song, "Ministry, May 1995, 5-9.

27　Frank A. Thomas, They Like to Never Quit Praising God-The Role of Celebration in Preaching (Cleveland United Church Press, 1997, 19.

28　Rock, 10.

## Chapter 3 Notes "How., Can I Apply Black Liberation Theology to Apartheid practices in South Africa"

1　James Cone, God of the Oppressed, (Seabury Press, New York 1975) p.178-179.

2　Ibid. p .214-215

3　Tom Skinner, How Black Is the Gospel, (J.P. Lippincott, Philadelphia 1970) p.11.

4　Allan Boesak, Apartheid IS A Heresy, (William B. Eerdmans Publishing Co; Grand Rapids 1983) p.1-2.

5　Ibid. p.182-183.

6   Ernie Regehr, Perceptions of Apartheid, (Herald Press, Scottsdale 1979) p. 211-212.

7   Gayraud S. Wilmore & James H. Cone, Black Theology, (Orbis Books, New York 1979) p. 489-490.

8   Virginia Fabella & Sergio Torres, Irruption of the Third World, Orbis Books, New York 1983) p. 193.

## Chapter 4 Notes "Oppression of African Americans/ The Willie Lynch Letter and the Making of a Slave"

1   Christopher P. Momany, Doing Good, (Abingdon Press, Nashville 2011) p.36-38.Used by Permission

2   Paul Ricoeur, Symbolism of Evil, (Beacon Press, 1967) p. 352

## Chapter 5 Notes "Theological Contributions of African Americans"

1   Carlyle F. Stewart, III, God Being and Liberation, (University Press of America, Lanham) p. 5-566, 77-127. Used by Permission

2   James Cone, Black Theology and Black Power. (New York: Sea-bury Press, 1969), p.31.

3   Ibid., p.17.

4   Ibid., 27.

5   Ibid., p. 45-49.

6   James Cone, Black Theology and Black Power. (New York: Sea-bury Press, 1969), p.31.

7   Cone, B.T. L., P.23.

8   Howard Thurman, Deep is the Hunger. (Richard Ind.: Friends United Press, 1951) p.80.

9   Howard Thurman, Jesus and the Disinherited. (Richmond, Ind.: Friends United Press. 1981), p.21.

10  Cone, G.O.P., P.196.

11  Ibid., p.219.

12  Ibid.

13  Ibid., p.217.

14  Ibid., 219.

15  Simone de Beauvoir, The Ethics of Ambiguity. (Secaucus, N. J.: Citadel Press, 1975) p. 97.

16  Cone, G.O.P., P.217.

17  Robert McAfee Brown, Religion and Violence. (Philadelphia: Westminster Press, 1973) p.20.

18  Cone, G.O.P. P. 217
19  De Beauvior, The Ethics of Ambiguity, p.83.
20  Cone, G.O.P., p.226.
21  Ibid., p. 227
22  Ibid., p. 228.
23  Ibid., p. 229.
24  Ibid., p. 228.
25  Thurman, Deep River and the Negro Spiritual Speaks of Life and Death, pp. 60-61.
26  Ibid., p. 62.
27  Ibid., 52.
28  Thurman, The Luminous Darkness, p.1.
29  Ibid., pp. 4-5.
30  Ibid., p. 6.
31  Richard Niebuhr, Nature and Destiny of Man, Vol 1., p. 16.
32  Thurman, Deep River and the Negro Spiritual Speaks of Life and Death, p. 55
33  . Rand, Atlas Shrugged, pp. 978-979.
34  Ibid., p. 979.
35  Samuel K. Roberts, African American Christian Ethics, (The Pilgrim Press, Cleveland Ohio) p. 3-99, 151-217.
36  Erskine Clarke, Wreslin' Jacob: A Portrait of Religion in the Old South (Atlanta: John Knox Press, 1979). See also Charles C. Jones, The Religious Instruction of the Negroes in the United States (Savannah: T Purse, 1842; reprint, New York: Books for Libraries Press, 1971).
37  Clarke, Wrestlin Jacob, 40-41.
38  See Genesis 3:8
39  Richard H. Popkin, ed., The Columbia History of Western Philosophy (New York University Press, 1999), 7.
40  Raymond Brown, Jesus, God, and Man (Milwaukee: Bruce Publications, 1967), 104-5.
41  Soren Kierkegaard, Training in Christianity (Princeton: Princeton University Press, 1941), 37 quoted in John Macquarrie, Christology Revisited (Harrisburg, Pa.: Trinity Press International, 1998), 14.
42  Adolph Holl, The Left Hand of God: A Biography of the Holy Spirit (New York: Doubleday, 1998), 6.
43  Geoffrey Wainwright, "The Holy Spirit," in the Cambridge Companion to Christine Doctrine, ed. Colin E. Gunton (New York: Cambridge University Press, 1997), 273.
44  Generally, when the three Synoptic Gospel writers (Mark, Luke, and Matthew) and Paul refer to the Spirit of God, the Greek does not offer a

definite article. This observation will have decided the importance when we note a shift in the book of John.

45  George W. Forell, ed., Christian Social Teachings (Minneapolis: Augsburg Publishing House, 1966, 1971), 51.

46  Clement The Instructor 1.13, in Forell, Christian Social Teachings, 52.

47  Clement The Rich Man's Salvation, in Forell, Christian Social Teachings, 54.

48  Robert M. Grant, The Bible in the Church (New York: MacMillan, 1948), 101; quoted in Jerry Wayne Brown, The Rise of Biblical Criticism in America, 1800-1870: The New England Scholars (Middletown, Conn.: Wesleyan University Press, 1969), 4.

49  See Erasmus-Luther, Discourse on Free Will, trans. Ernst F. Winter (New York: Continuum, 1990), v.

50  Jerry Wayne Brown, The Rise of Biblical Criticism in America, 5.

51  Jeffrey Stout, "Tradition," in Westminster Dictionary of Christian Ethics, ed. James F. Childress and John Macquarrie (Louisville: Westminster/John Knox Press, 1986).

52  Raymond A. Belliotti, "Sex in a Companion to Ethics, ed. Peter Singer (Oxford: Blackwell Publishers, 1991), 316.

53  Ibid., 317.

54  See Christine Gudorf, Body, Sex, and Pleasure: Reconstructing Christine Sexual Ethics (Cleveland: The Pilgrim Press, 1994).

## Chapter 6 Notes "Social Contributions of African Americans"

1  Arna Bontemps, Negro American Heritage (Century Communications, Inc, 1968), 17.

2  Ibid., p. 34.

3  Ibid., p. 35.

# BIBLIOGRAPHY

1.  Baldwin, James. Go Tell It On The Mountain. New York: Dell Publishing Co., 1953.
2.  Bontemps, Arna. Negro American Heritage. San Francisco: Century Communications. 1968.
3.  Boswell, John. Christianity, Social Tolerance, and Homosexuality. Chicago: University of Chicago Press, 1980.
4.  Carpenter, Delores. African American Heritage Hymnal. Chicago: GIA Publications. 2001. Used by Permission
5.  Cone, James H. The Spirituals and the Blues. New York: The Seabury Press, 1972.
6.  Dubois, W. E. Burghardt. The Souls of Black Folk. New York: Washington Square Press, 1970.
7.  Fenelon, Marge. Reveille for the Soul Prayers for Military Life. Liguori: Liguori Publications 2010.
8.  Gutierrez, Gustavo. A Theological of Liberation. New York: Orbis, 1973.
9.  Hayes, Roland. My Songs. Boston: Little, Brown, 1948.
10. Johnston, Mada. Songs of Zion. Nashville Tn: Abingdon Press. 1981.
11. McClain, William B. The Soul of Black Worship. Madison, N. J: Drew University, 1980.
12. Raboteau, Albert J. Slave Religion. Oxford: Oxford University Press, 1978.
13. Roberts, Samuel. African American Christian Ethics. Cleveland Ohio: Pilgrim Press. 2001.
14. Slade, Styne. The Darker Brother. New York: E.P. Dutton & Co., 1974.
15. Stewart, Carlyle. God Being and Liberation. Landham MD: University Press. 1989.
16. Thurman, Howard. Deep River and The Negro Spiritual Speaks. Richard, Ind.: Friends United Press, 1972.

17. Tillich, Paul. Systematic Theology. Vol. 1 Chicago: University of Chicago Press, 1951.

18. Walker, Wyatt Tee. Somebody's Calling My Name. Valley Forge, PA.: The Judson Press, 1979.

19. Whitehead, Alfred North. Process and Reality. New York: MacMillan, 1929.

20. Wilmore, Gayraud. "Ethics in Black and White," Christian, "Christine Century. 1973.

# WEBSITES

http://www.ministrymagazine.org/...african-worship-its-heritage-character-and-quality.html by R. Clifford Jones September 2002, Used by Permission

Ohio Coalition Against Apartheid. "Duration 1984-unknown existed in the late1980's and may have continued until 1994.

www.lojsociety.org

http://newsome.com/31019984/Detroit-police-beat-black-man-ran-traffic-signal/Video video archives https://www.youtube.com/watch?Video

Wikipedia The Free Encyclopedia

WWW.redtail.org Used by Permission